'END TIMES: According to Scripture'

Anyone browsing a Christian bookshop will be aware of the numerous publications about Bible prophesy and 'End Times' events. Occasionally among this stream of books, a gem arises that is of significant value for those who love to research this aspect of Scripture. This recent work, by Dr Charles Pallaghy, is one that I would recommend.

His book is not one that can be read like a novel, but is a compilation of his Biblical research, personal views and insights, (many of them new and challenging on this subject), that will inspire further examination as we watch our present world events unfolding.

The author has lived a dedicated Christian life, being led and inspired by the Holy Spirit during his continual years of Biblical research. For many of us who are Christians, we feel that the world is marching towards its final climax. Just as the Wise Men knew the time of Christ's first coming, we are encouraged to be among the WISE company, who read the Scriptures, study the signs and are prepared for His second coming.

Therefore, as the reader diligently processes the views contained in this book, through the sieve of their own personal Holy Spirit led life and in the light of a careful examination of Scriptures, I believe they will find great blessing and insight.

Phil Baird, September 2021

Retired Teacher/Pastor & Friend

Forest Hill, Victoria, Australia

To order additional copies of this book, contact:
Xlibris
AU TFN: 1 800 844 927 (Toll Free inside Australia)
AU Local: 0283 108 187 (+61 2 8310 8187 from
outside Australia)
www.xlibris.com.au
Orders@Xlibris.com.au

ISBN: Softcover   978-1-9845-0782-2
             Hardcover   978-1-9845-0781-5
             EBook   978-1-9845-0780-8

Print information available on the last page. An audio
book is under preparation.

Rev. date: 12/15/2021

END TIMES

According to Scripture

C Pallaghy PhD

My 'use by' dates

This subject matter requires the frequent citation of scriptures. To comply with 'fair use' requirements I have cited verses from a wide variety of translations.

"Though your Word contained the plan, they just could not understand"

(Lyrics from *El Shaddai*)

Contents

Synopsis

Much of our previous knowledge on end-times has been neglected by the church in recent decades. The younger generations have been missing out.

Topics of neglect include the central figure of the woman in Revelation chapter 12. When Jesus appeared to the apostle John, who was in exile on the island of Patmos, Jesus came with the words *"Write the things which you have seen and the things which are, and the things which must be after these"* (Revelation 1:19, KJV). By this time John was an old man and out of circulation.

Jesus first tackled the things that are; how the 7 churches had fallen into decline (chapters 2-3) and what John must do about it by writing to the 7 churches. Next, Jesus tackled the things which must follow hereafter. Therefore, everything that follows chapter 3 is meant for the future. Thus, the appearance of the symbolic woman, shining with the glory of the Sun in Revelation 12:1, depicts a future event.

Christians have been deceived to believe that she represents Mary, mother of God and queen of heaven, crowned with 12 stars, labouring to bring forth baby Jesus. Why would the risen Lord want to be born again, I ask? Certainly not, as will become apparent. She is a symbolic representation of the glorified bride of Christ labouring to bring forth offspring to the glory of God near the end of time. Her 'man-child', also a multiple, is immediately caught up to heaven. This group is the first-fruit of her labours with a great harvest of redeemed souls to follow. Offering of the first-fruit or the first-born, of man or beast, to sanctify the rest is a principle of God. At Passover Jesus was our first-fruit. His offering sanctified Pentecost when many were born again and filled with the Spirit.

Exodus 34:18-23 links the strict command of first-fruits together with the Creation and the three compulsory Feasts of Israel. **These three themes of God are inextricably linked – i.e. impossible to tease apart, as you will find throughout my book.** The Spirit and the bride say *"Come"* (Revelation 22:17). She and the Holy Spirit will be on a world-wide mission, but another woman becomes a formidable opponent.

The evil spirit within this woman, sitting on the beast with seven heads (Revelation 17), has been the archenemy of God's people for millennia. Israel has had to bow 7 times to world powers but, in the time of the end, Israel shall prevail (Genesis 33:3; prophecy of **"Jacob's trouble"**, Jeremiah 30:1-11). God renamed Jacob, the son of Isaac who was the son of Abraham, Israel because Jacob was given power with God (Genesis 32:28).

"And he carried me away, in the Spirit, into a wilderness: and I saw a woman sitting upon a scarlet-coloured beast, full of names of blasphemy, having seven heads and ten horns. And the woman was arrayed in purple and scarlet, and decked with gold and precious stone and pearls, having in her hand a golden cup full of abominations, even the unclean things of her fornication, and upon her forehead a name written, MYSTERY, BABYLON THE GREAT, THE MOTHER OF THE HARLOTS AND OF THE ABOMINATIONS OF THE EARTH. And I saw the woman drunken with the blood of the saints, and with the blood of the martyrs of Jesus. And when I saw her, I wondered with a great wonder" (Revelation 17:3-6, ASV).

She wantonly calls herself a queen but God will bring her down into the flaming pit (Revelation 18:7-8). The mystery of Babylon has religious origins whose basic philosophy is rebellion against the rule of God (Genesis 11:3-4).

Fear of having to deal with symbolism should not deter readers. To give us a head start, on several occasions the book of Revelation interprets its own symbolism. For instance, "The waters that you saw, on which the prostitute was seated, are peoples, multitudes, nations and languages" (Revelation 17:15, Williams Bible).

Enjoy your read with a cup

Foreword

The Holy Spirit revealed to Anna and Simeon that they would see the Christ before they died (Luke 2:22-38). The Spirit did not reveal the exact date so they waited prayerfully at the temple gates until the day came when Mary and Joseph finally arrived with baby Jesus for His circumcision to satisfy the Law of Moses.

This is one of the reasons why Caesar Augustus had them moved to Bethlehem, despite the hardship of travel from Nazareth, to be registered there because Joseph belonged to the house of David. In those days Bethlehem was called the city of David. This was according to God's grand plan so that they would be close to the Temple in Jerusalem and thereby fulfil prophecy (Micah 5:2; Malachi 3:1-6).

Would that kind of foreknowledge about His Second Coming be specific enough for you today? Only the Father knows the exact year and date, but that doesn't excuse ignorance. Ignorance was one of the major sins of Israel that God forgave the nation annually, but only once, on the Day of Atonement during the Feast of Tabernacles. The church is awaiting the fulfilment of the Feast of Tabernacles in the same way that Passover and Pentecost were literally fulfilled for the body of Christ. We need to wait expectantly for the Second Coming.

Jesus expects us to recognize the season of His coming. The Bible provides sufficient information for that, but not for us to calculate the exact year of the Second Coming! There are too many variables in our calendars and where exact cut offs between phases may have been. But the patterns are certain and set in concrete. God works in 'Weeks'.

Jesus said that we need to look for the signs of His coming and severely reprimanded the Pharisees for missing His visitation. They could forecast tomorrow's weather but failed to recognize the signs of His coming in preparation. Are we committing the same sin?

God has provided answers concerning the timing of His coming for those who dig deeper into the Word. Are you willing to come on that journey with me in slow, stepwise fashion by following these notes?

Charles Pallaghy PhD, July 2021, Mount Evelyn, Australia

Prologue

Because what I am about to share here might surprise or perhaps even anger some I need to establish first that I am in no way questioning the salvation of those who are in Christ. The born-again believer delights in His Word.

"So you will be saved, if you honestly say, "Jesus is Lord", and if you believe with all your heart that God raised Him from death….Everyone who calls on the name of the Lord will be saved" (Romans 10:9-13, CEV). **Of course, there is an essential sequel to that,** *"If we say that we share in life with God and keep on living in the dark we are lying and are not living by the truth. But if we live in the light, as God does, we share in life with each other. And the blood of his Son Jesus washes all our sins away"* (1John 1:6-7; James 2:14-26, CEV). We walk in the light as we obey His Word, *"Your word is a lamp for my feet and a light for my path"* (Psalm 119:105, GW).

When the disciples spent 40 days with Jesus, after the resurrection, they became born-again believers (John 20:22), but Jesus didn't want them to go out and spread the gospel just yet. He had more for them in store. A new phase lay ahead and they needed to be appropriately equipped. They needed something extra and Jesus didn't give it to them all in one package when they were born again. Unbeknownst to them He deliberately planned a delay of 10 days until He was ready to send them the Holy Spirit to be in them. He first had to return to the Father. The 10 days was also a test to see how many of the 500 or so who had seen Him after the resurrection would be prepared to wait even if they didn't know how long that would be. He wanted them to wait in Jerusalem until they became endued with power (Pentecost, the infilling or baptism of the Spirit). Until then the Holy Spirit was only with them not in them, strange as it may seem. The majority of them gave up and went back to their homes. The number **10** is Bible code for a test.

For hopefully good reasons churches may also have withheld studies on the book of Revelation until an appropriate time. The book of Revelation concerns things that Jesus considers essential knowledge for those heading into the end-times, hence His repeated strong admonitions to hear and keep the words of the prophecies contained in the book.

Churches have wanted to avoid confusion because many of the prophetic scriptures are still shrouded in mystery, hence the widespread diversity of interpretations that prevail. However, end-times are surely just around the corner, as I will show later on. Therefore, some ground work must begin to be laid to prepare us for what lies ahead. It can't be achieved overnight with a sermon or two. We should begin to tackle those things in Revelation that are already abundantly clear. However, we must also revisit important aspects in the Old Testament that shed light on end-time prophesies. Sadly, many of those foundations are missing or have simply been set aside as superfluous in the zeal to forge ahead and win new generations of Christians. The enemy has robbed the body of Christ for far too long (John 10:10).

Many might be put off and confounded by the difficult symbolisms of end-time events, as recorded in the books of Ezekiel, Daniel and Revelation, but of one thing we can be certain; they will have to dovetail into the reality experienced by the church of things foreshadowed by ancient Israel's Feast of Tabernacles, all the way from Trumpets to Booths, which ended the ecclesiastical (sacred) year in the Hebrew calendar. Passover and Pentecost were literally fulfilled in the church, **so must Tabernacles, the last of the three 'Feasts', also be fulfilled.** I will make this clearer later on.

A further confounding factor, as indeed is also the case for Genesis chapters 1 and 2, is that some of the chapters in the book of Revelation are not in strict chronological order. Nevertheless, none of these are an excuse for not familiarising our congregations with keys such as I am presenting here. They could become a starting point from which the Lord can unravel more and more over the next few years.

On June 3, 2021, the new Victorian president of the Australian Medical Association said that there has been a collective complacency in the nation over the past 6 months when the Covid virus could have been dealt a decisive blow. Putting Covid aside, the Lord highlighted the wording to me because the same could be said about the collective complacency over decades the way Australian churches have not dealt with themes I am raising in these notes.

Revelation is a book which God specifically designed for the end-times and hence is copiously coded with the number 7, to indicate that purpose, just like God uses the 7th day as the end of a week. Some of Daniel's prophecies were deliberately sealed for the end. Its mysteries were hidden even from the prophet himself (Daniel 12:4-9). The Lamb is able to open the book that has 7 seals (Revelation 5:1).

Admittedly, Revelation is a fearful book but it is at the same time a most glorious book for believers establishing that Jesus is triumphant. This book is tomorrow's newspaper. Even in the midst of the most horrible catastrophes the angel cries ***"rejoice you apostles and prophets"***. God wants us to rejoice because, with every page forward, we are closer to entering the glory of Paradise and to finally experience peace on earth and have our tears wiped away (in the Millennium).

The book of Revelation runs in parallel with the prophetic elements involved in the last of the three major Feasts of Israel instituted by the Lord - Tabernacles. The Feasts are a shadow of heavenly things to come and, therefore, **must** play out in the church age before the end. This is important because the Feasts are strictly chronological whereas the book of Revelation is not always presented in chronological order. The Feasts, therefore, serve as a sort of *Rosetta Stone* by means of which Revelation can be placed in better chronological order. The Rosetta stone allowed the translation of Egyptian hieroglyphs because the same text was also inscribed on the stone in Greek as well as in ancient Egyptian script (Demotic).

"Revelation does not end with judgement. Instead it provides a striking bookend for the entire Bible which begins in Paradise and ends in Paradise" (Rev Chuck Swindoll). Actually, as I will explain later, it really begins with the glory of the Lord and ends with the glory of the Lord. Judgement and correction play a major role in the book and this is what people detest. Perhaps it strikes one's conscience too much and we just don't want to know. It's like putting one's head in the sand hoping that it will go away. Moreover, the book of Revelation reads like science fiction with Hollywood-type aliens rearing their heads. But that is only symbolism used for our benefit. The beast, for example, is a person or persons, according to context, who exercises a beastly nature towards the people of God. Thus Jesus called Herod a fox because he was sly and couldn't be trusted. As another example, a beast with seven heads represents the same beastly nature dominating the governmental philosophies of seven separate kingdoms or eras. Horns represent 'power'. If they wear crowns it means that they are reigning and not playing 'second fiddle'. I hope that this will allay the fears of some readers. To give us a head start the book of Revelation sometimes even interprets its own symbolism. For instance, a sea or waters are people and nations,

"The waters you saw, on which the prostitute is sitting, are people, crowds, nations, and languages" **(Revelation 17:15, GW).**

The number seven stands for fullness or completion. That is why the book of Revelation, detailing the end-times, is filled with the no. 7: 7 lampstands, 7 stars, 7 churches, 7 seals, 7 angels, 7 plagues, 7 trumpets, 7 thunders, 7 vials, etc.

Are you confused by the symbolism of prophetic language and in God-given dreams? Be glad because so are Satan and the enemies of God. But these mysteries are being unfolded and revealed to us by the Holy Spirit. Have you seen *'Windtalkers'*, an American 2002 war film? During WWII, in the Pacific, the enemy could easily intercept military messages no matter what languages the signallers attempted to use. But they finally stumped the enemy by using specially trained Navajo, native Americans, whose tongue the opposition could not decipher. A 'turtle' in the Navajo tongue indicated a 'tank'. There was double encryption in effect. Revelation 1:20 has double encryption because one still has to understand who the angels are.

This breakthrough gave the Americans a massive advantage in the last stages of the war. I photographed their commemorative statue at Window Rock in Arizona while visiting a very good friend of mine, John. Satan and the stubbornly unrepentant, whose minds are darkened by the will of God, will never understand until it's too late,

"They knew God but did not praise and thank him …. their misguided minds were plunged into darkness. While claiming to be wise, they became fools" (Romans 1:21-22, GW). *"… 'To this day God has given them a spirit of deep sleep. Their eyes don't see, and their ears don't hear!' And David says, 'Let the table set for them become a trap and a net, a snare and a punishment for them. Let their vision become clouded so that they cannot see. …"* (Romans 11:8-10, GW).

I would agree that Revelations 1-3, the Old Testament, the four gospels, and the epistles are all that have been required to establish the kingdom of God on earth up to this point. **Jesus is enough, we sing and say.** However a new phase lies immediately ahead and its challenges will be super-enormous. God is preparing a bride in times of extreme duress but she needs to prepare herself despite the stress (Revelation 12:1-2, 19:7).

The revealing of the bride, world-wide, is the last major item on God's program before the Second Coming, as was also the case with Eve when the Lord made her from Adam only towards the end of the 6th working day during "Creation Week". **God is going to repeat the pattern.**

The Rev Hal Oxley warned, in his book on end-time prophecy, that not all Christians will be in the bride. As he said, "*Many choose to camp out early on their Christian pilgrimage*". Many are comfortably resting in their salvation and therefore have no desire to proceed into the meat of the Word. In his 2020 book, *Being: What God Wants You To Be*, he writes "*..the Word of God states that a believer's overcoming walk will necessitate traversing different stages*", the emphasis being on an **overcoming walk**.

The milk of the Word is pleasant and sufficient for many; it suits their daily routine (1Corinthians 3:2) but spiritually can put them to sleep like a baby. Not having a desire to mature is the danger. This attitude frustrated the apostle Paul (Hebrews 5:11). The apostle Peter admitted that what Paul brought to them was often difficult to comprehend but also conceded that we should try to understand those matters as they are important. Some people who misunderstood Paul's intentions twisted them to their own detriment (2Peter 3:16). A need to become mature readers of the Word, to prepare for end-times has been made abundantly clear in the book of Revelation and we have to discover what it is that we have to prepare,

"Let us be glad and rejoice and give glory to him; for the marriage of the Lamb is come and his bride has made herself ready" (Revelation 19:7, JUB).

Reading the Bible only at face value is like watching an iceberg without being aware that only 10% is revealed on the surface.

Mature readers search out the hidden revelations that go below the surface (the meat of the Word). A superficial understanding of Genesis chapters 1 and 2 is a prime example.

What is there to prepare corporately? The prayers of Jesus in John 17 and Paul's words in Ephesians 4 reveal much, but there is more to be found in the book of Revelation. There, Jesus puts an even greater expectation on believers.

It seems to me that we have entered the spiritual equivalent of the blowing of trumpets world-wide as many believe that we are entering end-times as I also do. The call (the purpose of the Feast of Trumpets, Yom Teruah or Rosh Hashanah, Leviticus 23:24-25) to get serious is before us if we look at Christianity world-wide.

Trumpets on the 1st of the 7th month were associated with the end of the summer fruit harvest in autumn which was followed by the latter rains (amazingly prophetic of end-times, Joel 2:21-32). The fruit was enjoyed in portable booths for **7** days after the Day of Atonement, lasting from the 15th to the 21st of the **7th** month. The Feast of Tabernacles then finished with a final day on the 22nd, the **8th** day of holy consecration, following the 7 days spent in booths (sukkahs). The number **8** has the meaning, in scripture, of resurrection and a new beginning (KJ Conner, e.g. The **8** souls saved on Noah's Ark).

Special sacrifices and prayers highlighted the entire period. I should also explain a matter that can cause confusion. The Feast of Tabernacles has three components each of them also called Feasts;

1. **Trumpets** (Rosh Hashana, the day of shouting and blasting with the shofar, *Yom Teruah*).
2. **The Day of Atonement** (*Yom Kippur*).
3. **Booths** (*Sukkot*).

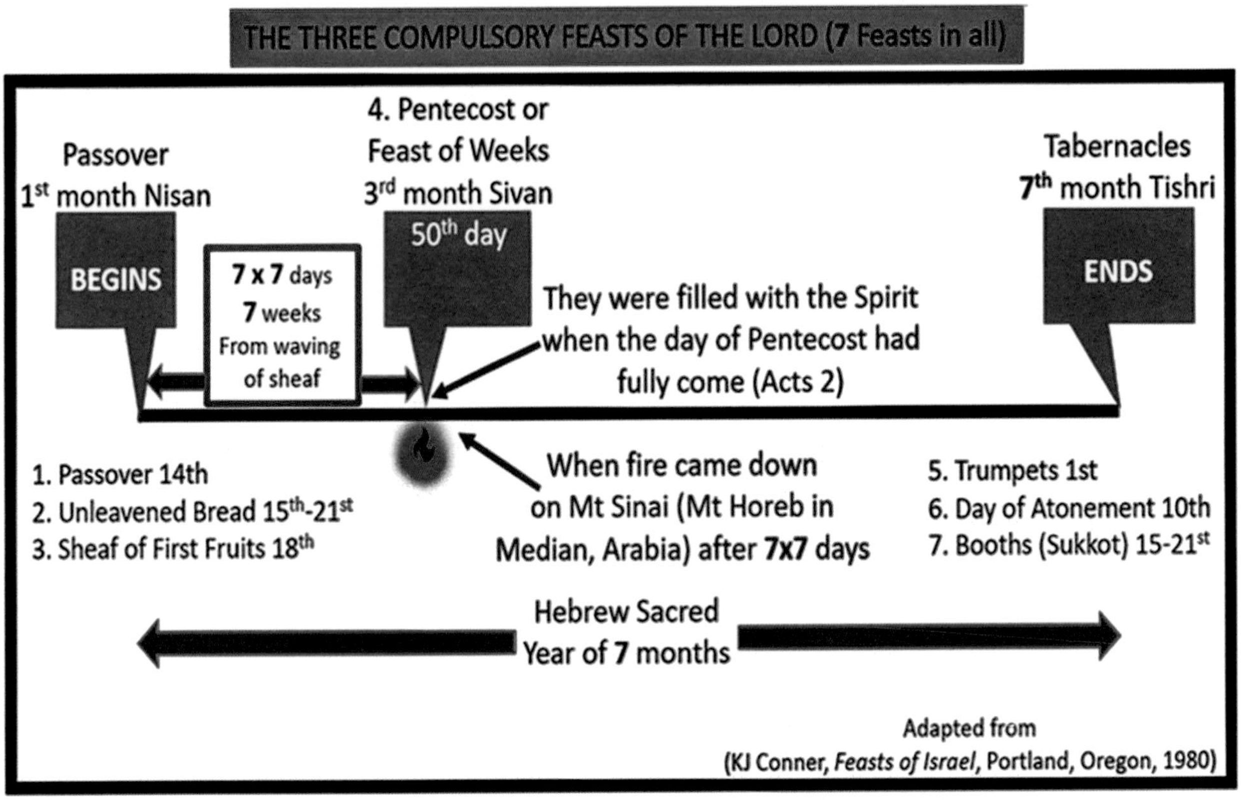

THE THREE COMPULSORY FEASTS OF THE LORD (7 Feasts in all)

4. Pentecost or Feast of Weeks
3rd month Sivan
50th day

Passover
1st month Nisan

Tabernacles
7th month Tishri

BEGINS

7 x 7 days
7 weeks
From waving of sheaf

They were filled with the Spirit when the day of Pentecost had fully come (Acts 2)

ENDS

1. Passover 14th
2. Unleavened Bread 15th-21st
3. Sheaf of First Fruits 18th

When fire came down on Mt Sinai (Mt Horeb in Median, Arabia) after **7x7** days

5. Trumpets 1st
6. Day of Atonement 10th
7. Booths (Sukkot) 15-21st

Hebrew Sacred Year of **7** months

Adapted from
(KJ Conner, *Feasts of Israel*, Portland, Oregon, 1980)

Unfortunately, Sukkot is often widely called Tabernacles, in the church and on the internet. Therefore, one must be acutely aware which feast one is referring to. It's the same problem with the name *Israel*, whether it refers collectively to all the tribes or only to the 10 northern tribes – the tribes lost in the diaspora, long before Solomon's Temple was destroyed, when the Jews were exiled for 70 years to Babylon. Another interesting matter is that not all Israel is comprised of Jews. Strictly speaking, Jews are Judahites but the term often also includes Benjamin and the priestly tribe of Levi who remained in Jerusalem with Judah following the split between the southern and northern tribes after the death of Solomon. Paul, the apostle, was a Hebrew and a Jew and also called himself a Benjamite. For added interest there were several people named Judas (e.g. Acts 1:13). Let's get back to our topic.

The 8th day, on the 22nd, completed the 7 month Hebrew religious calendar for the year. Because God's calendar or Grand Plan for the world is strictly synchronized to the feasts, as we have already seen with Passover and Pentecost, this infers that our resurrection and the beginning of the Millennium is going to be the last spiritually beneficial event that will be fulfilled in the church age. This will, hopefully, become clearer as you read on.

Another alternate name for Booths or Sukkot, the **Feast of Ingathering**, was so named because of the plentiful harvest in autumn of summer fruits such as grapes, olives, dates, figs and pomegranates which they were to enjoy as families

in their portable booths (huts or sukkahs) covered with foliage taken from four specified tree species. The sukkah could be built even on a roof top. The trees symbolically refer to the four faces of Jesus actively ministering within the body of Christ even as His chief attributes were also differently portrayed in each of the four gospels. We are called "trees of righteousness".

However, the primary emphasis in Sukkot was on fruits, but grains and seeds of various sorts were no doubt also eaten in stuffed cabbages and capsicums. **Many have taken Sukkot, quite logically, to symbolically refer to the ingathering of a great harvest of souls that the church will also experience at the time of the end through the ministry of the bride** (Job 42:12; Hosea 6:3; Joel 2:23; Haggai 2:9; Zechariah 10:1; James 5:7). There is much more that could be said concerning the sequence and details of the events.

"And the Spirit and the bride say, Come. And let him who gives ear, say, Come. And let him who is in need come, and let everyone desiring it take of the water of life freely" (Revelation 22:17, BBE). **Clearly the bride has a very active role in the ingathering of souls.** You can listen to the joyful singing around this verse by Messianic Jews in Israel by clicking on the thumbnail presented later in this book.

From what I have gathered from Revelation so far are: the endurance to continue to walk with God under growing intense persecution and social pressures (political and religious 'beasts' promising welfare and 'goodly Christian websites', Revelation 13) that undermine the Word of God and repetitive environmental catastrophes of unprecedented magnitude that will cause many timid hearts to fail and defect from Christ. These are its foremost warnings (Luke 21:26; Revelation 6:14; 11:19; 14:9-10; 16:21). Indeed, Matthew 13:24-30 tells us to expect weeds to grow up within the church. As you would have surely observed weeds can outpace leafy vegetables. Also, Revelation warns against cowardice in the face of the enemy (Revelation 21:8; Also Judges 7:3 and many other encouraging references such as 1Samuel 1:14-15 where Hannah, mother of the prophet, was misunderstood by Eli the high priest who had a rather sad end).

We see a proto-type of the end-time beasts in Absalom, an evil son of King David, whose rebellion David glossed over because of his grieving father's heart. In attempting to steal the kingdom and the hearts of men from his aging father, Absalom would kiss and kindly speak to all who came through the gates of Jerusalem and lamented that if only he were king he would fix their problems. Beware of preachers who are friendly at the expense of the gospel. So the people fell into the snare and shifted their love from David to Absalom (2Samuel 15:2-6). This nearly cost David his life. David was the Lord's anointed but, as so often is the case and will be so at the time of the end, people prefer to listen to deceiving voices instead because its less challenging and because they find it difficult to believe that good intentions could actually become evil in the eyes of the Lord (Numbers 15:32-36; Jeremiah 27:14; 28:15; 2Timothy 4:3-4).

The symbolism of the woman drunk with the blood of the saints, whose startling appearance the apostle John at first admired (Revelation 17:6; 18:24), is of the demonically inspired woman called 'Babylon' that opposes the woman of Revelation 12:1, 'the Bride'. Spiritual 'Babylon' overrides the Word of God and embraces the wisdom of the world. She influences governments, economics and the 'church' worldwide (Revelation 18:10-24).

When I asked a renowned physicist who claimed to be a Christian, an invited speaker at a local Church of Christ, why his view on the creation and the origin of life differed greatly from the Bible, he responded that the early portions of Genesis were written poetically to a primitive people who wouldn't have understood the intricacies of science we know today. The minister in charge and the congregation frowned at me for daring to challenge the speaker with the Word of God. Objective scientific evidence, such as available on my website (creation6000.com) and elsewhere, actually supports the biblical account of the creation and a young Earth.

Thus it becomes a battle between two desirable queens one desirable to the wicked and arrogant, the counterfeit, while Christ's queen, the bride, shines like the Sun, is filled with the glory of the Holy Spirit and is crowned with a leadership authority (Ephesians 4:11; Revelation 1:20, 12:1) of **12** stars, twelve being the number of authority.

The bride is desirable to those who worship the Lamb even unto death. She

stands on the moon, which is symbolic of Christ, the rock. The Sun, Moon and Stars are types of the Father, Son and the Holy Spirit (1Corinthians 15:41). As the pock-marked moonscape reflects the beams of the Sun in the night sky, so the marred body of the Son on the cross expresses (reflects) the glory and love of the Father. His beaten face was disfigured beyond recognition (Isaiah 52:14). All was Satanically inspired.

Thus it's a spiritual battle to the death between these two powerful women. One must win the other must die forever. One can liken it to a game of chess played patiently by the white side against a very aggressive black opponent. Each queen has a king over them but, as in a game of chess, the book of Revelation tells us that white has won through a brilliant sacrifice (Revelation 19:11-16).

Let us also learn something from a parallel in nature – first the natural then the spiritual, as the apostle Paul said. A queen bee is the only female bee in the hive that gets to reproduce. If two queens hatch at once they must fight to the death. The winner then opens other queen cells and stings the larvae inside to death. As it is in nature so it is in the spiritual. So it has been for the last 6000 years. Revelation 18 tells us which queen will win. Our hope is surely that we will qualify to be included in "the bride of Christ".

Please don't misunderstand me. By using the analogy of bee behaviour I am not advocating anybody to kill anybody at all but evil cannot and must not co-exist with Christ in Paradise. Years ago I attended the talk of a missionary who had just returned from PNG. He recounted how after his evangelistic crusade a local chieftain came beaming to him saying, *"I only have one wife"* to which the missionary replied *"how come"*? *"I killed all the others last night"*. No, I am referring to spiritual warfare to destroy the works of the enemy who has infiltrated the souls of men and women,

"For, though walking about in flesh, we do not war according to flesh. For the weapons of our warfare are not fleshly, but mighty through God to the pulling down of strongholds, pulling down imaginations and every high thing that exalts itself against the knowledge of God, and bringing into captivity every thought into the obedience of Christ" (2Corinthians 10:3-5, MKJV) - all through the love of God, of course.

The greatest battles for control of the mind are forecast in the book of Revelation. As a Christian it continues to amaze me how our destiny is dependent on the daily choices we make.

"Then I heard another voice from heaven saying, "Come out of her (Babylon)*, my people, so that you do not take part in her sins, and so that you do not share in her plagues"* (Revelation 18:4, NRSV). It is an admission by the Lord that many Christians reside at ease in spiritual Babylon and sit tight on past laurels. Babylon does not refer to present day Iraq.

Revelation is a book suitable for the end-times. Jesus, who sees the end from the beginning, the Alpha and the Omega, exhorts that those who read the words of this prophecy will be blessed.

> **Revelation repeats the word "blessed" 7 times in the book. Why? Because there are things in it that will equip the saints to walk through to the end as joyful overcomers and not as distraught victims.**

Satan knows full well that he is facing the end so he will pull out all reserves to destroy faith, to put Christians into a state of confusion, into conflict with other Christians or spiritual slumber so to speak. Apparent good works don't bother him as long as people are not doing the will of the Father (Matthew 7:21). He targets churches especially. The apostle Peter found that out a few times to his dismay (Matthew 17:4-5; Mark 8:31-33), so will others unfortunately (Matthew 7:15-23). Unfortunately, the spirit of Babylon is alive and well in some parts of the church today.

Caught unprepared and ill-informed some Christians will no doubt succumb and turn from their faith when they are no longer allowed to buy provisions for their families under the rule of the Antichrist, 666. This weakness, inherent in some Christians, was seen in news reports when groups were challenged by ISIS to convert to Islam or they or their children would die. Some succumbed and some died for their faith. Knowing this ahead of time and having a vision will fortify faith, even unto death (Proverbs 29:18; Revelation 6:11). **The tragedy is that no one need to be in this third group of Christians when masses will face similar options by the Antichrist who will be granted power, <u>by God</u>, to rule the world for the last three and a half years.** During these times the Antichrist, a person whose qualities will be admired by the rest of the world, will cause all those who do not worship him to be killed (Revelation 13:15). Those who surrender their faith will have their names removed from the Book of Life. The angel of God said so (Revelation 14:9-11). They shall be tormented together with the devil and all the wicked forever and ever.

People surely need to become aware that by the time of Revelation Chapters 12-13 <u>God will</u> divide Christians into three groups, an unwelcome fact one never hears about in church. In His love God's intention is to make Christians pull their socks up and become serious about their commitment to Christ. Currently too many are complacently just coasting along depending on the goodness of God. Chapter 11 of Revelation is clothed in "temple language" that will not make sense until one has studied the Tabernacle of Moses. One will need to understand Chapter 11 in order to understand Chapters 12 and 13. Thus we need to pay far more attention to the whole of scripture.

I am genuinely concerned that, unless the church faces this truth and begins to delve into the book of Revelation, many fellow believers will fall into the category of the third group, mentioned in Revelation 12:17 (Darby), namely, ***"And the dragon was angry with the woman, and went to make war with the remnant of her seed*** (the third group)***, who keep the commandments of God, and have the testimony of Jesus".***

*"And the beast was given a mouth uttering haughty and blasphemous words, and it was allowed to exercise authority for forty-two months. It opened its mouth to utter blasphemies against God....**Also it was allowed to make war on the saints and to conquer them.** And authority was given it over every tribe and people and language and nation"* (Revelation 13:5-7, ESV).

The 42 months or 3 ½ years are the final years of world history before the general resurrection of all believers past and present at the Second Coming of Christ.

The other two groups were previously, safely removed from the dragon's reach but God will allow the third group of Christians to face their consequences because they did not bother to make themselves ready by ignoring or belittling the signs of the times (Revelation 11-13). This is the season or hour, or time (*Hora*, Greek Lexicon) prophesied by Jesus from which the Lord will protect the faithful, *"You followed my command to endure patiently so I will keep you from the time of trouble that will come to the world—a time that will test everyone living on earth"* (Revelation 3:10,

ERV). Or, as in the more familiar NKJV, ***"Because you have kept My command to persevere I also will keep you from the hour of trial which shall come upon the whole world..."***.

This was not a word to the church at Philadelphia per se but a prophetic word into the future because it applies to a moment in time when the entire world will be tested whether to take on the mark of the beast or not. Nevertheless, Philadelphia had trials of its own which they had to endure. Philadelphia was a faithful church which Jesus did not rebuke.

What a horrible thought; the dragon (Satan) given authority to overcome them? Can you imagine yourself or your children, or grandchildren being caught up in that? It really is serious stuff, something the church is failing to address. It's no good saying we don't want to inspire fear. There is such a thing as the fear of God (Philippians 2:12). Do Christians really revere God and consider His Word holy these days? But God is gracious. He is giving the church time, world-wide, to address the situation some will have to face. God Himself defined this period in history before the Second Coming. **It is set in concrete.** God has warned us ahead of time. There is a preparation through the Word that needs to be done.

God is holy. His word is holy. Hear *"Holy, holy, holy is the Lord God Almighty who was, who is and who is coming"* (Revelation 4:8, KJV).

Quoting from George Warnock's book, *The Feast of Tabernacles* (1951), ***"If men choose to remain where they are in their Christian experience then this message is not for them. Thank God that they may eat of the manna that falls from Heaven and drink of the water that flows out from the rock, and receive healing and strength for their journey. But, sorry to say, they shall die in the wilderness and shall not see the good heritage of the Spirit"***.

Introduction

Let's first ask a question to get our focus right. Why did God create the universe and mankind in the first place?

Answer: To fashion a select and willing people from mankind into His likeness - a perfected "Bride" for His Son. The "Bride" is code for a huge group of redeemed people who have a loving and intimate relationship with Jesus, who obey His commands and are led by the Spirit, thus pleasing the Father (Romans 8:14; Galatians 4:6).

"For by Him were all things created that are in heaven and that are in earth, visible and invisible, whether they be thrones or dominions, or principalities, or powers: all things were created by Him and for Him" (Colossians 1:16, KJV).

For this reason He subjects the creation to futility and subjects mankind to the affliction of a fiery furnace to bring forth pure gold (the bride), and then will permanently discard any dross and scaffolding He used into hell (Satan, demons, the wicked and the faithless: God's instruments that forged our faith through many trials, 1Corinthians 5:5; 1Peter 4:12).

When a building is completed there is no further need of the scaffolding. It would surely spoil the building.

God's love is warm and gentle but, when He confronts us with His '*Agape*' love, it can be intimidating (Revelation 1:14-15). God is quickly forging ahead with His *"Grand Finale"* for world history and forewarned all of us, in many ways, to be prepared for His coming. Are we appropriately prepared? What does the parable of the 10 virgins teach? All these virgins (cleansed in the blood) thought they were appropriately prepared but five were turned away from the wedding. They had only presumed that they were ready. What about the man who turned up at the wedding of the King's son but was not appropriately dressed? Both parables carry the same message. What is Jesus telling us?

There is an excellent current analogy in relation to the 5 of the 10 virgins who did not have enough oil in their lamps. While they were away to buy some more Jesus shut the door on them. It's too late to get vaccinated once one develops serious Covid-19 symptoms. One needs a build-up of antibodies prior to exposure to the virus which is what vaccines are designed to do. Sadly many unvaccinated people die in ICU. It's the same when one remains unresponsive towards the Word that comes.

At His first advent Jesus came as the gentle Lamb, but in the Second Coming He will appear as the victorious 'Lion of Judah'. Jesus gave us a brief glimpse of His "Lion" nature when, infuriated, He quickly made a whip out of cords and then drove the money changers out of the Temple shouting at them (John 2:13-17). His disciples were no doubt dismayed to see Jesus in this state.

To those who carelessly suppose that the Lord's coming will be a great blessing the prophet declared, "***Woe unto you that desire the day of the LORD! To what end is it for you? The day of the LORD is darkness, not light***" (Amos 5:18, KJV). In the important parable of the 10 virgins five made a rushed attempt to buy oil for their lamps (Revelation 3:18). The other five couldn't help them because oil was a personal possession that they couldn't give away even if they wanted to. Too late to look into the Bible again, much too late to catch up! Too many lost opportunities over the years! Half of the virgins were cast into "Outer Darkness" (Matthew 25:1-13). As virgins, holding lamps, they were pure, had illumination, but were caught out unprepared despite the Lord expecting them to have been prepared. **The five were not excused. Imagine that!** This is likely to amaze many who think that Jesus is a fuzzy "sugar daddy" and all forgiving. They just haven't read about the other face of Jesus or have presumptuously chosen to ignore the warnings.

One such person was Thomas Jefferson, the famous US statesman, who also served as President and fought for religious freedom. He loved people, according to *Philia* love (brotherly love in Greek), but had no stomach for *Agape* love, the self-sacrificial and holy love of God. In fact he was so offended by some of the statements of Jesus that he cut and pasted, and even rearranged verses in the authorised New Testament, omitting statements he found disturbing. Jefferson believed that the Bible should be examined in the light of reason. He was a humanist as well as a Christian. The two can't mix. He printed his own version of the New Testament (*The Thomas Jefferson Bible,* available through *Amazon*). I saw his original cut and pasted version of the New Testament at the Smithsonian Institute in Washington DC. In the examples shown, taken from Wikipedia (public domain), he decided to alter "out" to "up" in Luke 6:12 which seems harmless enough, but the Greek word '*exerchomai*' does not mean "up". In addition, he cut out something from between verses 12 and 14, as is visible.

It has been my observation, over the years, that many, many Christians have done the same with the New and Old Testaments; not with printed versions but in their minds. It's difficult to argue reasonably with such people, even using the scriptures, because often they already have their minds made up. Such are those serving a god of their own imagination. I 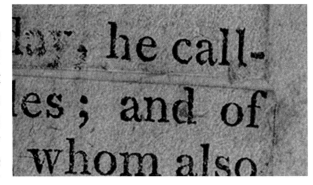 once tried to convince an eldership couple visiting from the UK that their board should not confirm a practising and self-confessed sexual offender to replace their deceased minister just because he was such a 'nice' and friendly person. But would they listen after I spent a whole night writing down all the scriptures that ought to have proven the matter to them? No, they did not.

Jesus is constantly giving us opportunity to be blessed, the word "*blessing*" appearing 7 times in Revelation. The number 7 signifies fullness or completion. Multitudes are currently at ease, busy with Covid and their daily routines, but refuse to listen to the trumpet call when it comes (Joel 2). They surely know that something is afoot; prophecies are being fulfilled at a rapid pace in Israel ever since the State of Israel was established in 1948. (Pockets of Israelite communities, identifying themselves as members of the 10 lost Northern Tribes, are streaming back to Israel from all over Asia and Africa, according to prophecy; there are currently in excess of 100 Jewish Messianic congregations in Israel who worship *Yeshua* - Jesus).

Multitudes of Christians are presuming on God's mercy and grace that they only need to pray for protection and healing, worship, participate in church activities and look after each other – and to evangelize but that's only the milk of the word. God wants more than that. The days are here where there is surely a call to be much more vigilant and to seek more in the Word.

Basic foundations

Are we certain that everybody's foundation, including those who have been around in church for years, is solid according to scripture? Is everybody filled with the Spirit? I wonder about that too. Just because one is born again there is no guarantee that they are also filled with the Spirit. Some may experience these two steps simultaneously others definitely do not.

We see that clearly illustrated in scripture. After all that Philip the evangelist had already achieved in Samaria the apostles still had to come from Jerusalem to fill believers with the Spirit (Acts 8:5-25). Simon the sorcerer had seen nothing like that in the company of Philip because none of those who had been converted and correctly baptized, in the Name, had also been filled with the Spirit. For many Spirit-filled Christians today their experience has been that it is a two-step process with as much as a year or more separating their two experiences. Some in our own congregation testified powerfully to that in my earshot. It was also my own experience. I really wonder whether believers have been challenged with that. I reckon that some only assume that they are filled with the Spirit and merge quietly with the others unnoticed. If that is indeed the case it's no wonder that they are satisfied having only the milk of the Word and quickly dismiss anything that is deeper. They have natural but only limited spiritual eyesight.

We even heard from an Australian couple recently, at a church function, that they were sincerely and enthusiastically doing Christian missionary work in Papua New Guinea for some time, sent out by their church from Australia, without ever having been born again until they were found out by a Spirit-filled native with enough guts to tell them so. The native caused them to repent and then baptized them by immersion in the local river to the amazement of the villagers looking on.

What's the purpose of being filled with the Spirit? The 120 in the upper room had previously spent 40 days with Jesus after His resurrection. They were believers and born again otherwise they would not have obeyed Jesus to wait to be endowed with power in Jerusalem. The resurrected Jesus would have made sure that they were believers. The new 12th apostle, to replace Judas, was appointed before the day of Pentecost (Acts Chapter 1). Only born-again believers would be able to do that but Jesus knew that they still required the experience of being baptized in the fire of the Holy Spirit. Up till then the Holy Spirit had been with them but not in them.

This two-step process was clearly illustrated with the new believers in Samaria. It has been mostly so ever since. This in no way excludes that some may experience both steps simultaneously, but we cannot assume that to be the case when people are born again. When a person was born again and filled with the Spirit simultaneously it is hard for them to fathom that it might be different for others. But the Word is clear.

Interestingly, the waiting period for the disciples in Jerusalem, before Pentecost, turned out to only involve **10** days, the number of testing in scripture (check it out). There is no record of Jesus revealing to them that God was actually testing whether they would obey. We only realize after an event that God was testing us, much as was the case with Abraham when he took Isaac to sacrifice him (Genesis 22:15-18). Of the more than 500 who had been in the company of Jesus, after His resurrection, only 120 obeyed and followed through. The others who had failed to endure were not found worthy to be included in the elect company on the day of Pentecost. When they saw the resurrected Jesus the 500 were, no doubt, eager to spread the news, but "hold on", said Jesus virtually, "I want you to be filled with the Spirit and His power before you are suitable for the task ahead". Would that also be an imperative command for today?

What about God's love, mercy and forgiveness? He is all of those, but: there is such a thing as being willingly ignorant or being unwilling to hear from God (Hosea 4:6; 1Corinthians 3:2; 2Corinthians 11:4; 2Peter 3:5, 16; 2Timothy 4:3-4; 3John 1:5-10). In some cases people may be too busy with their daily routines and set programs unwilling to make changes or make room for the extra effort needed (Matthew 22:1-14). The number **120,** in the upper room, was significant too because in the Bible it signifies 'the end of fleshly ways'. God isn't looking for people who will easily revert to ways of the flesh and worldly cares in the name of *philia* love. I wouldn't want their track record (Revelation 3:17). What is needed today is an administration of the Word that is appropriate for this end of time,

*"**Making known to us the mystery of His will, according to His good pleasure, which He purposed in Him to an administration of the fullness of the times, to sum up all things in Christ, the things in the heavens and the things on the earth, in Him**"* (Ephesians 1:9-10, WEB).

The spirit of unity

It suffices to touch on this subject by citing just one example from Indonesia. Jeff Hammond and his wife Annette have been good friends of ours from a long way back. Australians by birth they have been active ministering in Indonesia since 1974. I co-authored a book with Jeff in 1985 and subsequently he took me on a joint 'seminar' tour around parts of Indonesia to talk about God as Creator at various churches where he was welcome. I felt comfortable with him as my interpreter because I heard from the locals that his command of the Indonesian language is better than what most Indonesians are capable of.

He has prayed for at least two Indonesian presidents in the past. At his request an Indonesian destroyer was despatched to pick up donated goods from Vancouver following the devastation of Aceh by 15-30 m-high waves in the 2004 tsunami. He was also one of the pastors that ministered to Andrew Chan, a leading member of the 'Bali nine', who was eventually executed despite having been responsible, after his born-again experience, for the conversion of hundreds of inmates and guards at Kerobokan Prison in Bali. Jeff wrote up his recollections of Andrew in a book published in 2018.

Jeff came back to Australia during the Covid-19 pandemic in Indonesia and has been inadvertently in lockdown ever since. I attended one of his seminars, in June of this year, 2021, where one of his testimonies struck a chord in my heart.

In the first couple of waves of the Indonesian pandemic more than 100,000 Presbyterians fled to refugee camps and then were left destitute without any pastoral help from their church. Jeff, by now a prominent elder within the 20,000-strong congregation they run, heard about the situation as well as being told that his congregation had identified 32 Presbyterian pastors who were begging on the streets.

With some indignation he confronted the Presbyterian synod to get to the bottom of this dilemma. He was told that the Presbyterian Church was cashless and had no funds to support their pastors or give aid relief to their devastated church members. Speaking on behalf of his congregation, Jeff made an offer to pay the salaries of the 32 pastors for one year as long as they were redeployed to help out all of their languishing members on the streets and in the refugee camps.

Taken by surprise the synod asked how it was possible for Jeff's congregation to be so generous. Jeff responded, *"all of our members pay tithes as well as offerings"*.

Jeff thought it inappropriate, at that moment, to remind them about the enmity that had been targeted by the Presbyterians for years against his congregation for their doctrines on tithing and baptism by immersion.

The synod accepted Jeff's proposal and a little later asked him to organize their members to be taught about tithing and proper baptism. Therefore, through Covid-19, God not only brought their opponents to their knees but also opened a pathway for true unity to commence.

How much God loves us

I don't think we can even imagine how much the Lord loves us. God loved His creation and was grieved when Satan led Adam and Eve astray. Satan had marred the holy state of the creation.

I also don't think that the destroyer of mankind had any idea of the Grand Plan God had in mind to restore His creation. God was going to suffer and shed His own blood. That's how much God loves us.

But do we have any idea how much that cost God? I don't really think so. He jeopardised His own throne, His own being. If Christ had not succeeded there would have been no more trinity in the throne of God. God would have been plagued with the devil and his demons strutting back and forth gloating before the Father forever and ever. No, I don't think we can ever hope to fully appreciate the immense scale of His sacrifice once the Godhead agreed to choose His sacrificial Lamb even before He created the universe.

In God's eyes the Lamb was already slain from before the foundation of the world. This phrase is only found in the New Testament and appears **4** times (John 17:24; Ephesians 1:4, 1Peter 1:20; Revelation 13:8). As a master builder God implemented his Grand Plan with mathematical precision, involving **the number 7**, to be carried out with great patience and to tie together His blueprint for future events in world history and the final production of the 66 books of the Bible, which was a miracle in itself. *"All scripture is given by the inspiration of God"* (2Timothy 3:16, KJV).

"Josh MacDowell, a Christian apologist says: Here is the picture: 1,500 years, 60 generations, 40 authors, different walks of life, different places, different moods, different continents, three languages and writing on hundreds of conversational subjects. Yet when they are brought together there is absolute harmony from beginning to end...there is no other book in history to even compare to the uniqueness of this continuity" (quoted from the *Word for Today*, Vision Christian Media, July 2021).

The **number 4** has great significance in the code language that God has embedded in the Bible. The number **4** stands for "of world-wide significance". That is why we have the four corners of the compass, the four gospels and the four faces of Jesus, as I shall explain later.

God had to have a Grand Plan covering every possibility of Satan's intrusions because the risk, even to Himself, would have been great. Have we realized the enormous risk God took? I mean, failure could have split the Godhead. After all, Jesus was not only the Son of God but also the Son of Man with all our frailties. This is the Son in whom the Father is well pleased (Matthew 17:5).

Once the angels found out that God wanted to make man in His own image Lucifer rebelled, together with one third of the angels, being ignorant of the fine print added to the covenant God made with Himself. I can imagine, in the Spirit, Satan saying, **"What me? Look at my glory. Created only to be a servant to humanity? Never - no way, if I have anything to do with it. I will glorify myself instead and become like the Most High Himself"** (Ezekiel 28:11-19; Isaiah 14:12-14).

The fine print He missed was that God built into His plan a legal clause, a mysterious loophole that would be revealed to the court of heaven once Jesus had shed His blood. The mystery of the loophole was that it would allow Christ not only to rise from the dead but also to bring with Him all those who believed through His blood. He would rise with a great harvest of souls.

"... as Moses lifted up the serpent in the wilderness, so must the Son of man be lifted up that whoever believes in him may have eternal life. For God so loved the world that he gave his only Son that whoever believes in him should not perish but have eternal life. For God sent the Son into the world not to condemn the world but that the world might be saved through him. He who believes in him is not condemned; he who does not believe is condemned already because he has not believed in the name of the only Son of God" (John 3:13-18, CJB).

Are you familiar with the story of the brazen serpent (Numbers 21:4-9)? When Moses led the people through the wilderness, after God set them free from Pharaoh, the people found the way hard. At one point in their rebellion God became so angry that he sent a plague of slithering snakes through the camp. Many were bitten and died. Moses interceded and pleaded with God. God had great respect for the man so He commanded Moses to build a brass pole with a brass serpent twisted around it and to set it high in the ground. Everyone who was bitten could now come, look upon the pole and be healed. God had provided a way but some never obeyed the command to come and be healed. That explains why the medical fraternity often have symbols of a serpent coiled around a pole on their number plates.

The serpent was made of brass; brass or bronze always signifying the need for repentance (Revelation 1:15). That's why all the items in the Outer Court of the Tabernacle of Moses, as well as in the Temple of Solomon where the blood of animals was shed, were made of brass. The two massive columns guarding entry to the Holy Place, named Jachin and Boaz, were also made of brass signifying that without anointing and repentance one is not welcome into the Holy Place, as King Uzziah found out and became instantly leprous (2Chronicles 26:16-21).

So why have I shown the serpent in black? To signify that when Christ took upon Himself the sin of the world He became momentarily as Satan himself. ***"Yet the LORD was pleased to crush him severely. When you make him a guilt offering he will see his seed, he will prolong his days, and by his hand, the LORD's pleasure will be accomplished"*** (Isaiah 53:10, CSB).

How Jesus must have been tormented in soul when He was separated from His Father. ***" At three o'clock Jesus cried out in a loud voice, 'Eloi, Eloi, lama sabachthani'? This means 'My God, my God, why have you deserted me'"*** (Psalm 22:1 and Mark 15:34, NIrV)**?**

But by how much more does God love us? Consider galaxies in general. Dr Google estimates the number of stars (suns) that God created, in just the Milky Way galaxy, to be equivalent to twice the number of people who have ever lived on Earth. It comes to a staggering 100,000,000,000 suns like our own. It would take 200,000 years to cross from one end of the Milky Way to the other travelling at the speed of light.

In these two photos, by courtesy of Adrian Duncan, the Milky Way is viewed edge on. The panoramic shot reveals the curvature of the rim of our galaxy. Bright areas indicate a high concentration of suns (stars).

Galaxies are disk shaped. We are obviously located in one of the arms which is above the plane of the Milky Way. If that is the Lord's power over the natural creation why have you been worried that heaven might be too crowded for you in eternity? Note the other faint galaxies in the photo. That's how much you are treasured.

Here is a Hubble Camera shot with a **tiny pinhole** view of the sprinkling of galaxies throughout deep space. Consider the vast distances between them.

Despite an estimated quadrillion stars in the universe (10^{24}) the Word speaks of God having created life only on the planet Earth (Genesis 1 and 2). No amount of wishful

thinking has disproven that. In my 60 years of experience in science every hopeful piece of evidence, such as finding water and strange crystal formations on distant planets, has only turned out to be another 'red herring'. None of the radio-telescopes have ever received messages from 'extra-terrestrials'.

Take home messages concerning the cosmos:

1. It is amazing that astronomers seem to claim that there are roughly as many stars in the average galaxy as there are galaxies. At lower magnifications galaxies look like single bright stars. There is something about stars that is important to God concerning the blessing of Abraham, the Father of all who believe, summed up in what God said to Isaac and Abraham, *"I will give you as many descendants as there are stars in the sky, and I will give your descendants all of this land. They will be a blessing to every nation on earth, because Abraham did everything I told him to do"* (Genesis 26:4-5, CEV). The number of the stars in a single galaxy seems to be about twice the number of people who have ever lived.

2. The following shows the awesome power and generosity of God. In Psalm 147:4-7 and elsewhere the prophets say, *"He decided how many stars there would be in the sky and gave each one a name.*
   Our LORD is great and powerful! He understands everything" (CEV).
   He knows us by name.

3. I am not advocating that one day we shall become space travellers. I was just highlighting that God is powerful enough to fulfil all His promises when we look at the incredible reality of the cosmos, *"But, according as it is written, things which eye has not seen, and ear not heard, and which have not come into man's heart, which God has prepared for them that love him"* (1Corinthians 2:9, Darby).

Part I. God Appointed Seasons and Years (Genesis 1:14)

Part I discusses scriptures and concepts that reveal that the Lord's coming is very near. Many are asking questions about end-times without getting a satisfactory answer. This section also focuses on what might happen if we remain complacent with what we have already achieved, mirroring attitudes that were in the church at Laodicea. Many might haughtily assume that they will participate gloriously at the Second Coming even without appropriate preparation on their part. We would not be expressing *agape* love if we remained silent and allowed our brothers and sisters to continue in this manner. *"As many as I love I rebuke and chasten; be zealous therefore and repent"* (Revelation 3:19 KJV). Paul said to the elders at Miletus, on his final farewell from Ephesus, that he was passing all accountability over to them, ***"Wherefore I witness to you this day that I am clean from the blood of all, for I have not shrunk from announcing to you all the counsel of God"*** (Acts 20:26-27, Darby). Consider also the accountability of watchmen in ancient Israel (Ezekiel 33:1-9).

God does not work haphazardly. The mystery hidden from the beginning has now been revealed if we choose to look (Ephesians 1:9). God has a grand plan that He has ordained to accomplish and complete in Christ. He is staging a *"Grand Finale"* for His Son and He seriously expects us to be prepared.

"making known unto us the mystery of his will, according to his good pleasure which he purposed in him unto a dispensation of the fulness of the times, to sum up all things in Christ, the things in the heavens, and the things upon the earth; in him..." (Ephesians 1:10, ASV).

Like a railway network that has arrival and departure dates, and times so God has likewise a complex network of appointed times for all things that He has preordained (Revelation 9:14-15).

Jesus, the Lamb of God, was foreordained before the foundation of the Earth but He appeared only at the due time, as appointed by the Father (Romans 5:6; 1Peter 1:20). We shall discover why these appointed times had to be just right.

There are several examples when the Jews tried to kill Jesus but each time He evaded them because *"it was not yet His time"*. According to the will of God the apostle John was obviously not to be martyred as were the other eleven. Exiled on the island of Patmos for protection he still had a prophetic ministry to fulfil (Revelation 10:11). Amazingly, God shall even delay the end until the number of those still to be martyred are actually martyred (Revelation 6:11).

> Had Satan understood the full details of this plan he would never have incited the Jews to crucify Christ (1Corinthians 2:8).
>
> According to a Hebrew scholar the Old Testament was absolutely clear on this matter. Neither the natural man nor the devils can understand until it's too late. Satan is limited in his abilities because the prophetic word can only be correctly interpreted through the Holy Spirit (1Corinthians 12:10; 14:26).

Whether we participate in His majestic plan, and in what manner we might participate, is something that is for us to choose. The key parables of the seed (Matthew 13) explain all the potential possibilities laid down before us. His plan will proceed with or without you or me but, because of His great love, He dearly would want us to be actively included. Note the following:

God insisted on Moses to construct the Tabernacle precisely according to the instructions received on the mount as well as to follow the appointed times for the 7 components of the annual Feasts of the Lord comprising Passover (first fruits of the barley harvest), Pentecost (near the end of the grain harvest including wheat) and Tabernacles (the final summer fruit harvest in autumn). All these were to be completed **within the 7 months of the sacred calendar**. Seven is an important number because it is code for perfection or completeness in the Bible (e.g. The **7** spirits of God in Revelation 1:4; 3:1; 4:5; 5:6).

God determined that the Hebrew ecclesial (sacred) year consist of only 7 months

God works in prophetic sevens whether it is in weeks of days, of weeks, of months or years. He is the master and mathematical genius over agriculture, seasons and years, eternity and human history as we shall see.

Even the 70-year captivity in Babylon was based on the number 7 because the people had neglected to obey and rest the land in the Sabbatical years, in the 7th year of the week of years of the sacred calendar, for 490 years. This means that they wilfully refused to rest the land and not pick the harvest 70 times. Thus God punished them for one year in captivity for every Sabbatical year they had been negligent, a total of 70 years. Through the writings of Jeremiah the prophet Daniel became aware of this and began his prayers for the release of the Jews.

"in the first year of his reign I, Daniel, understood by the books the number of the years whereof the word of Jehovah came to Jeremiah the prophet, for the accomplishing of the desolations of Jerusalem, even seventy years. And I set my face unto the Lord God, to seek by prayer and supplications, with fasting and sackcloth and ashes" (Daniel 9:2-3, ASV).

On the subject of punishment churches don't want to hear the word because God does not punish they say. Discipline or correction is the politically correct term. I would ask this question therefore. Is a king, because of his habitual disobedience, who has his sons killed before his eyes and is then blinded and carried off in chains, being corrected or punished (Jeremiah 39:7-8)? Or, if we claim that we are now under grace, then I would ask this question: In the case of a married couple, who orchestrate a deliberate set of lies before the Holy Spirit and then immediately drop dead, one after the other before a stunned crowd, are they being disciplined or punished (Acts 5:1-11)? For discipline to be effective one would surely have to remain alive.

I and my wife were guests of a brilliant prize-winning academic friend of mine in Israel for two weeks who showed me his vast fruit plantations in the fertile valley downhill from the Golan Heights. He had become wealthy because their ripened fruits were the first to hit the shelves in Europe. Being a self-confessed and proud Hebrew I asked him whether he rested the land every 7th year according to the law of Moses. *"Why should I?"* he responded, *"I would lose so much money"*. He had exactly the same mind set as his ancient forefathers.

Because God's works occur in 'weeks' we can line them up for comparison and see beautiful patterns emerging. How could God have orchestrated all that? It is awesome. Not only are the patterns fascinating but the blessing is that they allow us to deduce things about God's plans that are not directly spelled out in the Bible. The patterns reveal the divine hand of God. Together with the undeniable design evident in animals and ourselves it has bolstered my faith in God over the years.

"The wrath of God is revealed from heaven against all ungodliness and unrighteousness of men, who hinder the truth in unrighteousness... For the invisible things of him, since the creation of the world are clearly seen, being perceived through the things that are made, even his everlasting power and divinity; that they may be without excuse: because that, knowing God, they glorified him not as God, neither gave thanks; but became vain in their reasonings, and their senseless heart was darkened. Professing themselves to be wise they became fools" (Romans 1:18-20, ASV).

Abraham, Isaac and Jacob were not privy to God's great timetable but **the mystery was revealed in part to Moses** when God reset the Hebrew calendar by making the 7th month of the civil calendar, Nisan (or Abib or *Aviv* in Hebrew meaning ears of barley) to become the first month in the ecclesiastical calendar. This was so that Passover, in the month of Nisan, would coincide with the beginning of the barley harvest in the Promised Land. God set Tishri to become the **7th** month in which was celebrated the "Feast of Tabernacles" bringing the Hebrew ecclesial year to an end. That God limited the sacred year to only **7** months and not to 12 months is crucial to this book so I don't mind repeating that fact! Tabernacles completed the sacred calendar of the annual cycles.

God determined that the Hebrew ecclesial year consist of only 7 months from the beginning of barley harvest in spring to the end of the summer fruit harvest in autumn. Why? This should crystalize in your mind more as you persevere to read on.

Thus Christ, our Passover lamb, would be seen as the first sheaf of barley (first fruits: a sheaf was waved before the Lord and became the property of the priests – us! (Leviticus 23:9-14) of many to be birthed later on the Day of Pentecost (3000 at the beginning of the wheat harvest, **7x7** days or **7** weeks after Passover). Pentecost was the 50th day.

Before the "Exodus of the Hebrews from Egypt", under Moses, God strictly specified an unblemished lamb to be taken on the **10th** day of Nisan (Abib), to be hidden from view in a pen for **four days** and then killed on the eve of the **14th** day. Its blood was to be applied to the door posts and lintels of every home (the vertical and horizontal strokes being prophetic of the cross). God also specified that its flesh be entirely consumed that night, both elements pointing to the wine and bread of the communion; the blood for atonement and the bread to heal our bodies (as explained by Kathryn Kuhlman who had an extraordinary ministry of healing between the 1940s and 1970s).

Moses obeyed knowing that any change of date would have severely angered God and nullified the *passing-over* of the death angel amongst the Hebrews in Goshen. Because they had no blood on their doors the first-born of all the Egyptians died that night including the first born of their animals. The Hebrews marched out of Egypt in an orderly manner tribe by tribe (Exodus 12:51) without any one being feeble or sickly (Deuteronomy 7:15) nor did their clothes wear out in the wilderness. Considering that they had toiled under forced hard labour that is a miracle in itself.

The coming of the death angel was the 10th of the 10 plagues upon Pharaoh and his followers, **10** being the code number of testing throughout the Bible. Pharaoh failed even this 10th test because soon after he drove the choicest of his chariots and army to their death in the Gulf of Aqaba in the Red Sea (See amazing documentary evidence including the true location of the mountain of Moses, Mt. Horeb in Median, Arabia, on a DVD by *Questar Entertainment*).

From the moment when sin entered in through Adam (4000 BC, as meticulously calculated from the Bible by Archbishop Ussher in 1650 and accepted by virtually all) Christ was also hidden from man's view for **four of God's prophetic days** (4000 years, Psalm 84:10; 90:4; 2Peter 3:8) until it was the appointed time for Him to suddenly appear (John 1:36) and pour out His blood for our salvation. **The apostle Peter admonished the church not to be ignorant of this important**

prophetic key, of 1 of God's days representing 1000 years on earth, for a proper understanding of God's timetable through world history (2Peter 3:8). Moreover, he talked about it in the context of the creation.

When Lazarus died Jesus deliberately delayed (John 11:4-7) and played out this prophetic event to reinforce the important principle of four days for our benefit (John 11:17, 39). Although, in their eyes, Jesus was four days late He was **there at God's appointed time** to revive Lazarus.

Taking the lamb on the 10th day in the days of Moses prophetically unlocks the mystery as to how long Adam spent in the garden before he sinned. After all, Adam had the potential to live eternally but that privilege was abruptly terminated when he disobeyed God and failed his test of absolute obedience by eating of the Tree of the Knowledge of Good and Evil (Genesis 2:17).

We first need to understand that the processes of aging and death were unknown entities until sin entered the world. In his fleshly, perfect state, in the Garden of Eden, Adam's body did not deteriorate nor age nor express sexual desires, but because of sin's curse on God's creation, Adam now began to age because he had rebelled against God. He subsequently sired children. In the resurrection we shall not be tainted by even the slightest sin, which is why Jesus is able to promise us eternal life.

The moment that Adam and Eve sinned God carried out His threat for them to die within the same day. So how long was God's "day" in Genesis 2:17?

One cannot tell from genealogy how long Adam had been alive before his disobedience because genealogy would only record how long he had been aging before he died. It cannot tell how long Adam had been living in an eternal, ageless state before he sinned. After all, that is what we believe in heaven: we shall never show signs of old age. We shall be eternally youthful perhaps with the appearance of a 30-year old. I am suggesting that because that was the age when Levites could enter into priestly service and it was also the age when Jesus began His ministry.

The absence of Adam and Eve procreating in their eternal state before the Fall is in keeping with the absence of procreation in eternity where, according to Jesus, we shall be like the angels in that regard (Mark 12:25). We just have to accept that even though it seems to make no sense in the case of Adam and Eve. Eternity is a totally different state of existence.

"But of the tree of the knowledge of good and evil you shall not eat, for in the day that you eat of it you shall surely die" (Genesis 2:17, ESV). This is most surely a death threat on the physical body. How can it be understood any other way? They had to die the same day, within 1000 years. The biblical proof comes later in the book of Genesis from the ages at which people died from

natural causes. None of the fabulously long-lived patriarchs made it to 1000 years. Methuselah approached the ceiling of the limit most closely. He reached 969 years. Nobody made it to 1000 years or beyond. In prophetic language, God reckons 1000 years to be one day just as the apostle Peter said. Peter emphasised that we should not be ignorant of this fact, in 2Peter 3:8 in the context of the creation.

The 1000 year ceiling will only be surpassed in the 1000-year Millennium and beyond. Those who have been supporting the man-made doctrine of 24-hour days, for the six days of creation, have had to do a lot of fancy verbal footwork to cover their tracks and they succeeded. I have heard it spiritualized, that in Genesis 2:17, God only threatened a moral death of some kind. Yet such people are adamant that they believe the Bible. Moral death was one of its consequences too because now Adam and Eve were stained with sin for the first time since their creation.

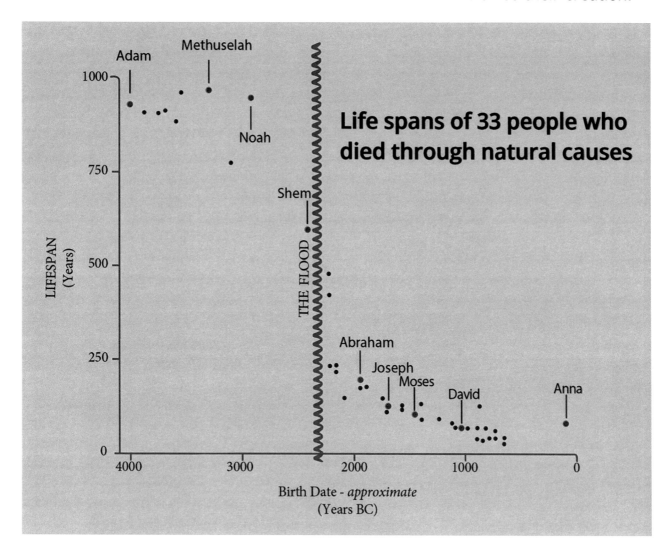

When one takes that together with the admission by the same people that the early church fathers knew that the days of Creation Week represented 6,000 years of prophetic earth history with a 7th millennial rule of Christ (personal communication, CEO of a parachurch, 2021), a fact that the proponents of the 6 literal days of creation do not wish to promote. Their motive to exclude eschatology, since it does not fall into their scientific expertise, doesn't seem right. Their argument is that it does not necessarily imply that the creation week also consisted of 1000-year prophetic days.

What is the pitfall which is snaring millions of Christians? Carnal reasoning and ignoring what the whole of scripture has to say by concentrating only on Genesis 1 and 2 and Exodus 20:11. The Jews deny the trinity using the same faulty carnal reasoning by quoting "*Hear, O, Israel. Jehovah our God is one Jehovah*" (Deuteronomy 6:4, MKJV) while ignoring that the God who created in Genesis 1 and 2 was **Elohim**, a plural word in Hebrew. If God was literally one why didn't the Hebrew scriptures use the singular **Eloah**? God is only one in the sense that there is perfect harmony of purpose and love within the Godhead. When will the church wake up?

Scripture records that Adam had been aging for 930 years before he died. Ignoring how long he may have been alive in his prior eternal state we would nowadays claim that he died when he was 930 years old. The process of ageing and dying is absent when we are in a totally sinless state, as was the case with Adam was until the day he sinned. Adam's age is therefore only reckoned from the moment he sinned. Thus, after he had sinned, Adam's life span fell short of **1 prophetic day equalling 1000 years**; neither did any of the other patriarchs manage to live through one of God's prophetic days. God's threat was coming true. The curse affected the whole of mankind through Adam's DNA (1Corinthians 15:22). DNA somehow carries the code for life span, everything else being equal.

It's the DNA that determines that the typical life span of a flowering annual plant is only 1 year whereas a bristlecone pine can live up to 6000 years. It's all pre-coded and regulated in the DNA molecule in the same way that we code programs digitally for computers to perform specific tasks. Annual plants are genetically programmed to die after they flower and set seed. They must die. Once they flower the process cannot be reversed no matter how well you may take care of it. God has done the same with mankind.

The horizontal axis of my graph (page 37) should more accurately read "Approximate birthdates from the time that Adam sinned, obtained from Young's Analytical Concordance of the Bible. Adam's creation was much earlier but he only began to age from an 'age of zero' at approximately 4000 BC, as meticulously calculated by Archbishop Ussher". The archbishop only had the lifespans of people in a cursed world at his disposal.

From the moment that sin and death entered the world until now almost 6 of God's prophetic days have passed, i.e. 6000 years. The practice of altars and shedding of blood began from the day when Adam sinned. Before evicting Adam and Eve from the garden God shed blood for their sake. It was the first shedding of blood on earth. God clothed them in fresh, blood stained animal skins (Genesis 3:21). The skins were not the garments of cavemen, but a symbolic covering of forgiveness through the foreshadowed shed blood of Jesus Christ. **God had begun His work of redeeming mankind from sin despite their sinfulness.** The ritual of sacrificial burnt offerings and outpouring of blood had begun, which is why God was pleased with the offering of Abel but had no respect with the offering of Cain who brought vegetables and the sweat of his brow to the altar for his burnt offering (Genesis 4:1-5). Cain committed the first murder out of jealousy.

When God destroyed the entire world, because they had corrupted His creation with violence, He saved Noah and his family on the Ark. Before God shut the door on them, from the outside (Genesis 7:16), the Lord had brought an extra number of 'clean animals' onto the Ark to be used for sacrifices later on (Genesis 6:20; 7:2-3, 8; 8:20-21). When they came out of the Ark, Noah immediately resumed his earlier practices and built a sacrificial altar to please the Lord. The building of altars and shedding of blood, in anticipation of Jesus shedding His blood on the cross, continued all the way to

Calvary. We are now covered by the blood of Christ. God has been working redemption for almost 6000 years since sin entered in.

Abel's sacrifice was acceptable because of the blood. He first had to kill the sheep or goat for the burnt offering. Of course, any blood sacrifice from Calvary onwards would be an abomination in the sight of God because it would deny the once for all sufficiency of the blood of Christ, ***"He has no need to offer sacrifices every day like high priests do, first for his own sins and then for those of the people, since he did this once for all when he sacrificed himself"*** (Hebrews 7:27, ISV).

At the resurrection we shall meet Adam and Eve and all those who had sacrificed by faith the blood of bulls, goats, sheep, pigeons and doves. Joseph and Mary, being poor, only brought a pair of doves (or perhaps pigeons) to the altar at the circumcision of Jesus, **one for a burnt offering and the other for a sin offering** (Leviticus 12:8; Luke 2:24).

"... under the Law almost everything is cleansed with blood, and without the shedding of the blood there is no forgiveness" (Hebrews 9:22, ISV).

Jesus fulfilled every detail, according to the letter of the Law, even though neither Jesus nor Mary, nor Joseph had committed sin through this birth. Adam had been commanded to procreate but, after the Fall, procreation and birth had a sinful nature attached to it so new mothers had to be redeemed under the Law of

Moses. As I will explain later it has something to do with the loss of blood during the birthing process. That is certainly not the case under grace (Hebrews 13:4).

Jesus similarly allowed Himself to be baptised by John even though He had nothing to repent about (Matthew 3:11; Acts 19:4). John the Baptist did not understand why Jesus, the Lamb of God, would want to be baptised unto repentance. By faith we understand that Jesus never sinned because He had the Spirit of God overshadowing Him at all times, even in Mary's womb. He was born of an incorruptible seed by the word of God (Luke 1:35; 1Peter 1:23).

Because Jesus fulfilled every jot and tittle of the Law Satan had no claim on the body of Jesus. His body saw no corruption. Even though Jesus had taken the sin of all humanity upon Himself, and the sins clung to His blood like oxygen does, the blood poured out onto the ground into forgetfulness. Thus the soldier who pierced Him played an important part in the process.

The miracle is that if we choose to believe in Jesus as our saviour then our sins are retrospectively transferred into the blood that went down the drain long ago, so to speak. It is amazing that by the grace of God we can claim forgiveness by faith. Those that choose not to believe by faith do not have their sins included in the blood that was poured out. Therefore their sins remain. They will die in their sins. It's absolutely amazing that Jesus encouraged us to believe for our prayers to come to pass according to our faith, with the proviso, of course, that it is according to the will of the Father. What we choose to believe is crucial! God ordained a spiritual law that it would be so.

Faith and repentance are great mysteries that fortunately Satan never understood. The mystery of substitution by innocent blood atoning for the guilty was made clear by the sacrificial rituals on altars throughout the Old Testament. Laying hands on the sacrificial animal transferred the sin from the guilty onto the animal's shed blood. This is why the gentile Christians were forbidden to deliberately eat blood (Acts 15:29); the Jews didn't have the same problem. They already knew that they were forbidden to eat free flowing blood, hence practising Jews only eat Kosher meats that have been drained of blood (***"The life of the flesh is in the blood"***, Leviticus 17:10-14, KJV). I can understand why that should be physiologically true because, in the natural, blood carries oxygen to the brain, but why it should be so spiritually remains the hidden mystery of God. Well, the short answer is that God created blood with all its required attributes, physical and spiritual.

Whether we fully understand the spiritual mechanisms involved in atonement is irrelevant. We leave that to God. The important aspect immediately relevant for my purposes is that **God has been working atonement by substitution through the transfer of sin into innocent blood** ever since the disobedience of Adam and Eve. It is the work of the Father and repentance of the heart that is the key to a successful transfer of our sins. No repentance leads to no forgiveness (Matthew 6:12-15). The apostle Peter insisted on repentance on the Day of Pentecost (Acts 2:38).

I shall share a vision that was part of a communion message presented at a large Melbourne Church. It's relevant to all of us, I believe. The vision which she saw is absolutely stunning. On this day Hazel Stoke suddenly saw herself facing Jesus hanging on the cross. In the vision she drew close to Jesus and passed through Him to emerge as a brilliant, white figure on the other side. All her bits of dirt and failings had clung to Jesus as she passed through His body. Jesus acted as a 'filter' absorbing all the dirt. Let it be so with all of us.

Thus we can say that God has been working to redeem mankind for the past 6000 years or so, 6 of God's prophetic days ever since Adam first sinned. Knowing that a 1000-year rest in Christ lies ahead of us and an uncanny feeling that we are approaching the end (Revelation 20:6) it's beginning to look as though God is going to repeat the pattern established in the week of creation, the Creation Week: six days of God's work followed by a day of rest (the Millennium) - more on that later. We shall call this the **Redemptive Week of God**. We could also call it the 'Week of Restoration of Man'.

Weeks are very important to God, whether they are weeks of days, of weeks or of months, or years, as used in the Bible. Perhaps we are beginning to get an inkling of why God determined that the religious calendar for the Hebrews should only consist of 7 months and not 12. Thus, using God's language, the yearly Hebrew sacred calendar lasts only **a Week of Months (7 months)**. God is in love with the number 7.

When in God's timetable did Adam and Eve actually sin?

Through the command given to the children of Israel to take a lamb for themselves on the **10th** day God openly revealed, yet still cloaking His Grand Plan in mystery, that on the **10th day of world history Adam and Eve had failed their test in the Garden of Eden and that a lamb was immediately needed!** This was all preordained – it had to be to fall into God's amazing mathematically based and most holy plan. It was the appointed time to let Satan loose to tempt the world and to begin the age of altars and blood sacrifices to counter the corruption Satan introduced into the world. The day of testing is what the number 10 signifies in the Bible, either for good or for bad. Sin entered the world on the 10th day of world history as can be deduced from the instruction given to Moses for the first Passover instituted in the land of Egypt.

Why did God allow mankind to fall into sin? The answer is that He doesn't want robots or slaves, *"Yes men or women",* in heaven. Overcoming our trials and temptations through faith and repentance demonstrates our voluntary love and loyalty towards God.

We can't blame Adam and Eve for their failure because we would have surely committed the same, **"for all have sinned and fall short of the glory of God"** (Romans 3:23, KJV); Paul directed this statement to Spirit-filled people. We are still capable of sinning but we are not condemned (Romans 8:1). On our confession and repentance God immediately forgives.

The lambs apprehended on the **10th** day of Nisan in Egypt and then hidden for **4 days mirror the 4000 years in world history** from the first entry of sin until Calvary, from about 4000 BC to almost 2000 years ago when Jesus was crucified. Jesus was hidden for 4 of God's prophetic days as illustrated below.

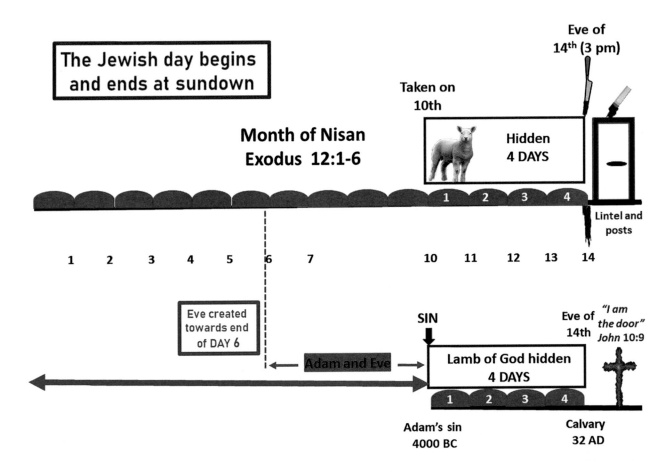

God's grand plan was hidden until an appointed time to be revealed by the Holy Spirit. Thus Satan, because he could not interpret types in prophecy, remained blind to the means by which he would eventually be defeated.

Interpretation of prophecy is a gift of the Holy Spirit. It does not come by scholarship. God had no intention to share that revelation with Satan. Satan even missed the crucial type of Jesus in Isaac when an angel restored Isaac to Abraham by substituting a ram for Isaac (Genesis 22:1-14). God's grand plan will be developed further as you read on.

As is evident from the diagram on page 50, my scriptural analysis and the pattern of God allows 6000 years for the creation of the world including mankind followed by a day of rest, the first millennium of 1000 years.

That Adam sinned, at approximately 4000 BC, was meticulously researched and made commonly known to the modern church by Archbishop Ussher only in the 1650's. Our understanding of the scriptures, much of which was already believed by the early church fathers, has been steadily unfolding and more rapidly ever since the great Pentecostal awakenings at the turn of the previous century such as at 'Azusa street', and elsewhere in the world, which grew out of much prayer and fasting. Great biblical understanding was gifted to giants such as Pastor W.H Offiler at Bethel Fellowship International (e.g. "*God and His Bible or the Harmonies of Divine Revelation-plus a Bible Study Chart*", 1946, available on Amazon amongst many others). Other scholars such as KJ Conner and WW Patterson have been building since on their foundations. God is constantly clarifying our understanding of the scriptures just as mankind is constantly getting better at unravelling the secrets of nature. Is God so small as to lag behind? This is exactly why the apostle Paul exhorted all to study the word because in it there is much reward.

"Do your best to present yourself to God as an approved worker who has nothing to be ashamed of handling the word of truth with precision. However, avoid pointless discussions. For people will become more and more ungodly and what they say will spread everywhere like gangrene. Hymenaeus and Philetus are like that" (2Timothy 2:15-17, ISV).

Should the question of the duration of days in the creation account and God's Grand Plan, based on a system of 7's, not be decided by examination of the whole of scripture? Even as I am proceeding to do step-wise here, and not just by a superficial understanding of Genesis Chapters 1 and Exodus 20:11?

Similarly to what George Warnock expressed in his book, on the Feast of Tabernacles, if people choose to remain where they are in their Christian understanding then my message is not for them. Thank God that they have found Christ through scientific approaches and continue to receive blessings but, as for me, I prefer to follow the leading of the Holy Spirit. King Jehoshaphat of Judah made a grave error when he turned his back on the prophet Micaiah, the son of Imlah, and fell in league with the king of the northern tribes of Israel in Samaria to join him in battle against the enemy (1Kings chapter 22).

Even while writing this book I saw a vision in my mind about a high conical tree in the distance that stood within a fenced area. It was laden with glistening fresh fruit.

I couldn't shake the vision away. The vision kept returning ever more strongly over the next few days. Then one morning when I woke up a few days later I eventually understood. The Lord was telling me not to think that the message I have is for everybody's taking. It is reserved for those who come through the door and ask. That gave me peace because I was becoming aware that not everyone would take this book to heart.

Why else was the Holy Spirit given to us if not to lead us into all truth? *"When the Spirit of truth comes, he will guide you into all the truth; for he will not speak on his own authority, but whatever he hears he will speak and he will declare to you the things that are to come"* (John 16:13, RSV). Does this excite you? What this means is that the Holy Spirit reveals a new way of looking at scriptures that weren't previously understood. The apostles didn't understand everything that Jesus spoke into their ears. Their illumination often came much later. I am applying that to what I am bringing here too. Pray and He will reveal it to you too! These truths will not remain secrets the closer we approach the end. They will reverberate around the world.

"For the earth shall be filled with the knowledge of the glory of the Lord as the waters cover the sea" (Habakkuk 2:14, RSV, and Isaiah 11:9).

Christians have misunderstood

Millions of people have misunderstood that they must believe that each of the days of the creation were solar days of 24 hours. The volume of the Bible does not support such a view. In fact, analysis of Genesis chapters 1 and 2 reveals that the Hebrew word for day *"YOM"* refers to four different periods of time in these two chapters alone. Unfortunately, this belief has become firmly entrenched in Christendom which has brought much joy to the enemy because it numbs belief in the prophetic word of God. What I present in this book is verified by the whole of scripture.

That solar days were not involved is verified when we look at the whole of scripture. It is the only place in scripture where we are told not to be ignorant (KJV). The apostle Peter was adamant when he was talking with the creation on his mind,

"But do not forget one thing, my dear friends! There is no difference in the Lord's sight between one day and a thousand years; to him the two are the same" (2Peter 3:8, GNB). And,

"A thousand years to you are like one day; they are like yesterday, already gone, like a short hour in the night" (Psalm 90:4, GNB).

"… surely people are worse! They live in houses of clay built on dust. They can be crushed as easily as a moth! From dawn to sunset people are destroyed. They die—gone forever—and no one even notices. The ropes

of their tent are pulled up and they die before gaining wisdom" (Job 4:18-20, ERV).

Are people being destroyed within 12 hours? Is this not a poetic use of 'morning' and 'evening' as also used in Genesis chapter 1? For example, as we would say in English, *'The dawn of a new era'* or *'She was in the evening of her life'* (Oxford English Dictionary). I would question commonly held dogma that the use of evening and morning in Genesis chapter 1 strictly only refers to a 24-hour day.

There was no Sun for the first 3 days so solar days did not exist during that period (Gen 1:14-18). There was no Moon either, the Earth was held up on nothing in empty space (Job 26:7). The days of creation were 'prophetic' days as explained in the text.

Moreover, consider this: Read Genesis chapter 2 carefully and imagine yourself in Adam's situation. Adam and Eve were the last of God's creation on day 6 according to the strict chronology given in Genesis chapter 1. Adam also had to be put into a deep sleep for Eve to be fashioned from one of his ribs, not just any sleep. Considering all that Adam experienced and what God was expecting him to do would the latter portion of a 12-hour day have been sufficient for all of that?

Notwithstanding that, before putting Adam into a deep sleep to make Eve, God not only commanded Adam to give names to every living creature that walked on the ground or flew in the air, but Adam actually completed the job (Genesis 2:19-20). Did God use a fast moving belt to swish them past Adam to make snap decisions or did God allow Adam time to observe and name them according to the sounds they made or according to their behaviour, as indigenous people are inclined to do all around the world? Indonesians tend to name animals according to the sounds they make while biologists generally tend to name them after their behaviour or appearance, e.g. funnel web spiders, sloths, spiny anteaters and woodpeckers.

After being so busily occupied Adam was also supposed to be suddenly yearning for a partner of his own. It stretches the imagination beyond belief that all this could have been completed in a 12-hour or even 24-hour day. There would not even have been time for God to introduce Himself to Adam and have fellowship with him. God did not create Adam to be an obedient robot but as a person to have fellowship with.

Without contradiction, the Bible in its entirety supports the days of creation being of 1000-years duration, but it's hard for well-intentioned huge organisations trying to uphold the Bible to backtrack on long standing commitments made in their constitutions. It reminds me of the time when the Ark of the covenant was being returned to Israel but the oxen stumbled and one of the priests, Uzza, who tried to protect the Ark, was struck dead for daring to touch the Ark which was always carried on poles. Uzza's response was a work of the flesh. King David became afraid and was greatly displeased with the severity of the Lord and wouldn't come near to the Ark for months after that (1Chronicles 13:5-14).

It would be enormously embarrassing to have to concede on a major theological error which has 'shoehorned' young Christian minds, as well as the minds of an innumerable number of pastors, in the many journal publications which have been very admirable in proving a young Earth. However, none can claim to prove literal 24-hour days for the six days of the creation. It is all based on the supposition of a superficial reading of a few scriptures without reference to the prophetic elements of the Bible. The Word is internally consistent and can hold its own. I have to make a stand for the truth. I cannot deny the scriptures. That's my challenge to all who read this book.

Was God just making empty threats when he said that in the day that they eat of the tree they shall surely die? The whole of scripture verifies that they certainly died within the one prophetic day of 1000 years, both 'spiritually' and bodily, not as some dogmatically claim that they died only spiritually in that 24-hour day and that's the end of discussion on that matter, as far as they are concerned. The long lifespans of the early patriarchs were put deliberately in the Bible as clear evidence for us to realize that every 1000 years on earth is reckoned by God as one day according to the prophetic language God uses.

Furthermore, following the description of the six days of creation in Genesis 1, Genesis 2:4 reads, **"This is the history** (or 'generations' in other translations) **of** *the heavens and of the earth when they were created; in the day that the Lord God made the earth and the heavens"* (AMPC). Are we now to understand that God made all these things in 24 hours? As stated earlier Genesis chapters 1 and 2 reveals that the word for day (YOM) is used for four different periods of time.

I also view Exodus 20:11 as being prophetic days, *"because in six days Yahweh made the heavens and the earth, the sea and all that is in them, and on the seventh day he rested. Therefore Yahweh blessed the seventh day and consecrated it"* (LEB). God used the pattern of the week of years (7000 years) of the creation to be mirrored in His law regarding the practical and social working week of 7 solar days.

I have one last question for those who wish to discredit the 1000-year prophetic days: Why did God have to put Adam into a deep sleep before He made Eve? Why didn't God just snap His fingers to make her? Parachurches assume He must have done that to create everything else within the 24 hours available each day, the entire universe, for instance, on day 4.

This surely is one more clue of many in His Word that God uses time and processes and not just brief commands in the first six days of the creation. "Let there be light" (Genesis 1:3) was not just a simple matter of throwing on a light switch. I highly recommend that readers listen to session 10 of Jeff Hammond's YouTube series on *"Jesus wants His Church back"* which also includes material on what the early church fathers and the Jews believed. I have placed a link on my home page (creation6000.com).

The first light, in Genesis 1:3, did not come from suns (stars) even as the light in the New Jerusalem will not depend on a sun or a moon. The Sun and the Moon were only created on day 4. Revelation 21:23 and 22:5 make it absolutely clear that the light will come from His own glory. Thus the Bible starts with His glory and finishes with His Glory. He was and shall ever be the light of the world.

"He who has ears to hear let him hear" (Matthew 11:15, KJV). The Holy Spirit says come and let us move on.

Questions by a prominent CEO of a science-based parachurch about my time chart

I would like to share the argument put to me by the CEO of a prominent parachurch organization. You may have similar questions about my proposal.

1. He had a serious problem with my proposal for the time chart of world history in this book which requires that Adam lived for a very long time before he sinned. His question basically boiled down to this, 'Why would God give a command to Adam and Eve to multiply when they would only be able to fulfil the command

a very long time later when Cain was born, after they had sinned? Surely they were fertile and did not have the bodies of angels. They would have had intimate relations over all that time in the Garden and birthed thousands of children before Eve was tempted, according to your time scheme'. **I responded by asking a similar question as to why, in God's mind then, was the lamb slain from 'before the foundation of the world' when man hadn't even been created yet nor sinned"** (1Peter 1:19-20; Revelation 13:8)?

The obvious answer in both cases is that God foreknew that one day man would be able to procreate and that man, one day, would also sin and depend on the blood of the lamb for forgiveness.

One needs to be constantly reminded that we have a miracle working God. For the 370 days that Noah spent on the Ark God suspended all the natural instincts of the wild animals (Genesis chapters 7 and 8). In Daniel chapter 6 God stopped Daniel from being eaten by the lions, but God didn't stop the ferocity of the lions when his accusers were thrown to the same lions the very same day. We have another example how God ceases natural instincts in the story of the old prophet, the lion and the donkey in 1Kings 13:11-34. The lion became docile, after first having killed the disobedient prophet, and the donkey did not run off. Both the donkey and the lion remained faithfully guarding the body at the intersection until another prophet came to claim the body for burial. This amazing miracle was witnessed by many which is how the prophet heard about the dead prophet lying on the road guarded by animals that were natural enemies.

Furthermore, believe it or not, there was something sinful about birth and the menstrual cycle to do with the flow of blood which is why such women had to be atoned for with a burnt offering (Leviticus 12:1-8). Therefore, are we going to be ruled by our human reasoning or by the word of God? Have faith in the word and believe that God kept Adam and Eve busy doing other things. After all, there will be women and men in Paradise for eternity without any further procreation or sexual desires. Hard to imagine but that's what Jesus said (Matthew 22:30).

2. He also wrote that his organization was well aware that the early church fathers knew that the days of Creation Week represented 6,000 years of prophetic earth history with a 7th millennial rule of Christ, but that did not necessarily imply that the creation week also consisted of prophetic days. I queried in my mind why that should therefore be excluded as an option.

It makes me wonder why such object to my proposal that the scriptures promote that all the days of the earth are couched in prophetic terms. Would it open floodgates against 24-hour days in the creation?

Jesus used prophetic language Himself several times in ways in which a literal meaning must be excluded, including eating His flesh and blood in order to have life

(John 6:53). That turned many off and they stopped following Jesus because they failed to grasp His prophetic use of language. They didn't even bother to inquire. Can we be like that too?

Other examples are:

- He replied, *"Go tell that fox, 'I will keep on driving out demons and healing people today and tomorrow, and on the third day I will reach my goal'"* (Luke 13:32, NIV). He was prophesying that there will be two days of the church age followed by another day, the Millennium. He wasn't talking about His three days in the grave. How could He have been healing and driving out demons from the grave before His resurrection?

- *"Then Peter came to Jesus and asked, 'Lord, how many times shall I forgive my brother or sister who sins against me? Up to seven times'? Jesus answered, 'I tell you, not seven times, but seventy-seven times'"* (Matthew 18:21-22, NIV). Is this gobbledygook? Not at all. Jesus was referring to Daniel's 70-week prophecy (70x7, Daniel 9:24-27) which covers the entire period between the command of Darius in Babylon to rebuild the Temple in Jerusalem through to the end of the 2000-year church age. Jesus was effectively telling Peter that Christians always have to forgive. It is interesting that God put a prophetic word *'seven times'* into the mouth of Peter, something that he probably didn't ever learn as an uneducated rough fisherman.

- How on earth did the early church fathers know about a 6000 year plus a 1000 year millennium time-line if they did not believe in the principle of a restoration week and in 1000-year prophetic days? Most of us only see that in hindsight because of the meticulous work on genealogies by Archbishop Ussher, in the 1650's, that the time span between Adam's sin and Christ was established to be 4000 years.

- Amazingly, I was also asked why I should argue that days 1-3 were not necessarily solar days (on the basis that Genesis states that the Sun, Moon and stars were only created on day four). Why he rejects this suggestion out of hand puzzles me. Others have pointed this out too!

Finally, at His trial, and I believe this relates to how Genesis Chapters 1 and 2 are read superficially, they accused Jesus of having said that if this temple were destroyed he would rebuild it again in three days (John 2:19-21). All his hearers thought that He was talking about Herod's Temple and thought Him crazy, but Jesus meant something totally different. He was talking about the temple of His body. This is only another instance where hearers totally misunderstood Him. Jesus often spoke in code. The Bible speaks in code also.

The principle of 'two weeks' of years, 2 x 7 years

The principle of the week was most holy; anyone found working on the **7th day, the Sabbath,** was to be stoned to death without pity (Numbers 15:32-36). All of these strictly specified and holy demands have spiritual significance concerning appointed seasons and times throughout world history. However, as I have intimated earlier, there are actually two separate weeks of years that overarch world history: **the Week of Creation** and **the Week of Redemption** (or **the Week of Restoration**), each having its' **own 7th day** as a Sabbath day of rest. Hebrews chapter 4, if read carefully show that there are two 7th days of rest, one in the past and one still to come for the redeemed.

Christ, the last Adam (1Corinthians 15:45), was wounded for us **5** times with iron (by a spear and three nails) and **7** times overall (with stripes and thorns), the numbers in code signifying grace and perfect love respectively. It is through the free flowing blood from his side that Jesus purchased the bride, as also was the case with Eve when she was fashioned from one of Adam's ribs. Perhaps this is why when women experience free flowing blood, which is not Christ's for the purpose of redemption, that they need to be atoned for. Eve was presented to Adam by the Father; similarly, the bride will be given to the Son by the Father (Matthew 22:2). Can you sense a pattern emerging?

"Yet the LORD was willing to crush Him and He made Him suffer. Although you make His soul an offering for sin He will see His offspring and He will prolong His days, and the will of the LORD will triumph in His hand" (Isaiah 53:10, ISV).

SIX DAYS OF WORK — 1000 Year Sabbath — EVE

1 2 3 4 5 6 7

DAYS OF CREATION WEEK
6 x 1000 years

In the first week God worked for six 'prophetic' days of 1000 years each to create and then rested on the 7th day. Eve was made towards the close or 'evening' of day 6. When Adam explored the Garden of Eden he noticed that he didn't have a partner as did all the animals. God anticipated his thoughts and so provided Eve as a helper for all the tasks given to him and to overcome his loneliness. **Eve was the last of God's first creation** as we can see in this time chart (Genesis 2).

Compare this with the time when Christ was pierced to bring forth the church. Blood and water gushed forth, speaking of the atonement, baptism and the Spirit, to fashion the desired 'second' woman (the bride yet to be perfected) from His side towards the end of the 6th day which is just around the corner (6000 years from the entry of sin ie. from 4000 BC as estimated by Ussher). I wish to highlight, once more because this is important, the parallel between Christ being speared in His side with Adam whose rib was removed from his side to fashion Eve (Genesis 1:27; 2:15-23). These patterns of creating brides are undoubtedly God inspired!

*"**But one of the soldiers pierced his side with a spear and, at once, blood and water came out**"* (John 19:34, CSB). Note that in Zechariah 12:10-14, concerning the piercing of Christ, it mentions the word 'wives' 5 times. God is emphasizing that as the blood and water was gushing from his side it prepared the way for the bride. Five is the number of grace in the Bible (KJ Conner, *Interpreting The Symbols and Types,* 1992).

The heavenly pattern continues. Just as Jesus was conceived in Mary by the Spirit so will the bride have been conceived through Jesus by the Holy Spirit. Both Jesus and the bride are heavenly, though living in the flesh they are not of the flesh! It is refreshing to think that neither Jesus nor His bride are of the flesh. In the bride we shall see perfection (Ephesians 5:27) and the end of all fleshly ways. The bride will have died to herself and is totally surrendered to Christ. That is a big ask if you and I want to participate in the bride that is currently being fashioned. You and I can't do it. It has to be achieved by the Spirit of God.

Let's develop our theme further. As I have already mentioned God appointed for Himself a second week, referred to as the **"Week of Redemption"** or the **"Week of Restoration"**, in which He has already been working for almost 6 prophetic days (6000 years since the Fall) to undo what Satan had done and to redeem and restore man to perfection on Earth as we see promised in Ephesians.

"And he gave the apostles, the prophets, the evangelists, the shepherds and teachers, to equip the saints for the work of ministry, for building up the body of Christ, until we all attain to the unity of the faith and of the knowledge of the Son of God, to mature manhood, to the measure of the stature of the fullness of Christ" (Ephesians 4:13, CEV). This greatly annoys Satan. He has been working overtime to make sure that Christians don't believe this scripture. It's something He wanted for Himself but without Christ his archenemy (Isaiah 14:14).

Hebrews 4:4-11 not only talks about the day of rest, immediately following the creation, but also that **there remains a 7th day of rest for the people of God**, a future Sabbath, in which Jesus and His people will be able to rest for 1000 years on a cleansed earth (the Millennium, Revelation 20:2-7). This is what the early church fathers and followers of the Jewish Talmud also believed as admitted by the CEO of the parachurch organization. The first four days of 4000 years involved altars and sacrifices for atonement which became abominable to God after the crucifixion of Jesus (Hebrews 10:6-10). The next 2000 years under Christ is the church age or the age of the Holy Spirit. Then follows the 1000 years of the millennium making it a total of 7000 years or a 'week' of 1000-year days, a total of 7000 years; 6000 years of God working redemption and the next 1000 years of rest. Applying the Millennium to our time chart we obtain the following:

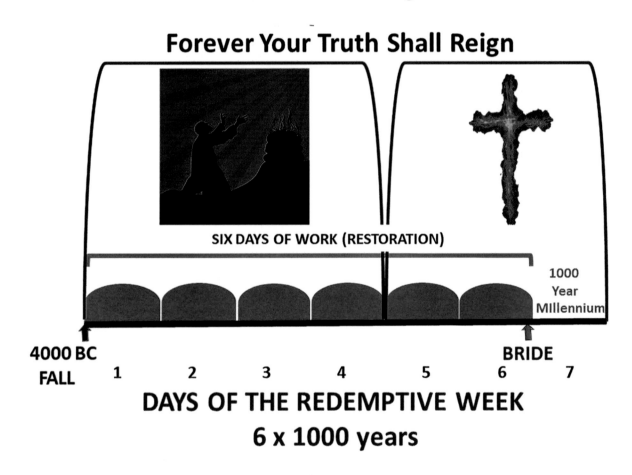

Forever Your Truth Shall Reign

SIX DAYS OF WORK (RESTORATION)

1000 Year Millennium

4000 BC
FALL

BRIDE

1   2   3   4   5   6   7

DAYS OF THE REDEMPTIVE WEEK
6 x 1000 years

We are not yet speaking of the New Heaven and the New Earth which comes after the Millennium when the Earth and the present universe shall be dissolved (Revelation 21:1; 2Peter 3:7-13). The infinitely awesome God will create something even much more superior for the faithful to enjoy.

Jacob laboured two weeks of years for beautiful Rachel

The Bible is brutally honest about failures in people's character, which gives the rest of us much hope. Jacob was such a person. Though he was unscrupulous in his younger years God watched over him and led him to a victorious life eventually changing his name to Israel. He became the father of the 12 tribes yet still had to face much trouble and heartache in his own home.

After deceiving his father Isaac and cheating his brother Esau out of his inheritance, and following his parent's advice, Jacob fled to his mother's family in Syria to seek a new life away from his brother. There he fell in love with the beautiful Rachel, the daughter of his mother's brother Laban. He struck a deal with Laban that he would serve him for 7 years if he was allowed to take her hand after that, but Laban had a cheating heart too, as Jacob would find out soon enough.

It is amazing to read Isaac's final blessing after the way his own son Jacob had deceived him, ***"Isaac called for Jacob and blessed him...'You are not to marry any of the Canaanite women... Go to Paddan Aram to ...Bethuel, your mother's father, and get yourself a wife from there from the daughters of your uncle Laban. May God Almighty bless you...and increase the number of your descendants ... May He give to you and your descendants the blessing of Abraham so that you may take possession of the land where you are now living, the land that God gave to Abraham"'*** (Genesis 28:1-3, GW).

This is, of course, what the fight for the State of Israel and Palestine is all about. Muslims believe, according to the Koran written 610-632 years after Christ and thousands of years after the book of Genesis, that the inheritance of Canaan belongs to Isaac's half-brother; Ishmael, who was born to Sarah's maid the Egyptian woman Hagar. However, the ancient land of Canaan was promised to Israel (Jacob) the son of Isaac. Isaac was the miracle son promised to Sarah by Elohim (Hebrew plural for God, singular is Eloah) when she was too old to bear children (Genesis 17:15-21). It was Isaac who was taken to Mt Moriah (site of Solomon's Temple in Jerusalem) to be sacrificed (Genesis 22:2).

God had been watching over Jacob all along guiding his steps because God had great plans for him. Laban, a type of Satan, robbed Jacob of his first attempt to get the wife of his dreams. Jacob was cheated because, on the night of the wedding, Laban swapped Leah for Rachel and it was too late by the morning to reverse the situation. Jacob didn't like her looks because she had 'weak eyes'. Laban argued that he had to marry off the eldest first. Jacob was so desperate to have Rachel that he promised to work another 7 years for her (Genesis 29:17-29).

God rewarded Jacob with so much success in his work that Laban and his sons became bitterly envious and tried to cheat him of his wages on several occasions but, each time, God thwarted their evil intentions. In the end Jacob had to flee from Laban taking with him his two wives, children and livestock.

Because the Spirit of God had been hovering over Jacob's life, guiding his every step, we can see a beautiful pattern emerging from his two weeks of years of labour to obtain his two wives. **The diagram below** shows how Jacob's two weeks of years parallels with the two weeks of years God has struggled against Satan to seek the wife of His desire for the Son of God – the bride of Christ. Note the pattern of 7's that God is so concerned to retain. Weeks are extremely crucial in the plans of God from Genesis to the book of Revelation. The entire religious year of Israel was embodied and completed within a week of months (7 months), from Nisan to the month of Tishri. God deliberately did not work according to a solar calendar of 12 months as we are accustomed to do. This is so, so important for us to realize. Maintaining a pattern of 7's means everything to God! This fact deserves to be tattooed on our foreheads.

Jacob's life ran in parallel with the first Adam's earlier experience who ended up, during the Creation Week, with Eve, a bride who soon was proved to have a weak character. There was a weakness in Leah also that repelled Jacob. This is one of the reasons why he became so possessively in love with the two sons Rachel bore once Rachel passed away, Joseph and Benjamin. Leah's children often had impure motives which is another one of the reasons why they couldn't stand Joseph and sold him into the slavery (Genesis 37). The dove in the diagram represents the Holy Spirit watching over the desired outcome over these lives.

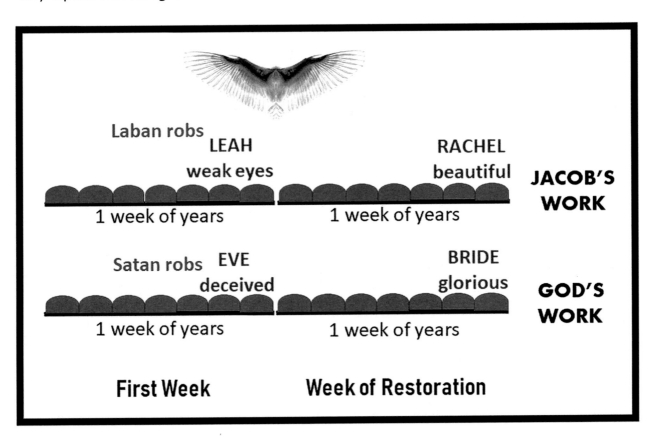

The overall picture

The overall picture is that, from the moment that sin entered the world and the process of aging began in Adam until the present time, almost 6000 years have passed, i.e. 6 of God's prophetic days. At the end of the 6th day God will no longer work, which means that there is no further salvation beyond the 6th day. The Holy Spirit will be taken from the Earth when people will have to endure the last 3 ½ years under the rule of the Antichrist (Revelation 11:2; 13:5). Once the opportunity for salvation passes no one will be able to complain that God was not fair,

"For God's grace, which brings deliverance, has appeared to all people" (Titus 2:11, CJB).

God will not be working to redeem on the **7th day** (Hebrews 4:8-11) because it is a time of rest and because the time limit for the final number of the redeemed has been reached; not the number of the redeemed but the time when salvation will no longer be available.

The generation we live in probably cannot comprehend God's idea of rest on the 7th day of the week. Nowadays we can visit shopping centres and restaurants or go to movies on Sundays. It was not so when Australia was still considered a "Christian" country. Our youth would have been so disappointed with the restrictions we had to face on Sundays in the 1950's and earlier. The streets were 'dead' apart from church goers.

At the very end of the 6th day there will be no more grace for the wicked; only judgement will await them at the return of the "Lion of Judah". CS Lewis depicted this very well in his novel *"Narnia: The Lion, the Witch and the Wardrobe"*. At the time of the Second Coming the whole world will see him and the signs of His coming (e.g. Amos 8:9 and Revelation 18). They will grieve and quake indicating that there is a progression to the Lord's physical coming; it won't be in a flash of time,

"...When he opened the sixth seal, I looked and there came a great earthquake; the sun became black as sackcloth, the full moon became like blood, and the stars of the sky fell to the earth as the fig tree drops its winter fruit when shaken by a gale. The sky vanished like a scroll rolling itself up and every mountain and island was removed from its place. Then the kings of the earth and the magnates, and the generals, and the rich and the powerful, and everyone, slave and free, hid in the caves and among the rocks of the mountains, calling to the mountains and rocks, 'Fall on us and hide us from the face of the one seated on the throne and from the wrath of the Lamb; for the great day of their wrath has come, and who is able to stand'"? (Revelation 6:12-17, NRSV). Nobody will be able to miss this advanced sign of the end times!

However, the wicked will be destroyed by the brightness of His coming. We see a glimpse of how it will happen from the description of the resurrection that took place in the garden,

"… there was a huge earthquake. The angel went to the tomb…and rolled the stone away… The angel was shining as bright as lightning…The soldiers guarding the tomb were very afraid…They shook with fear and then became like dead men" (Matthew 28:2-4, ERV).

At the physical return of Christ all the redeemed, whether dead or alive, will take on their resurrection bodies and be ushered into the 1000-year Millennium. What a wondrous time awaits us,

"They (the resurrected redeemed) **lived and reigned with Christ for a thousand years! The rest of the dead did not live until the thousand years were up. This is the first resurrection… No second death for them! They're priests of God and Christ; they'll reign with him a thousand years"** (Revelation 20:4-6, MSG).

We read further in the book of Revelation that our restful bliss will be momentarily interrupted at the end of 1000 years by the resurrection of the wicked, the **second resurrection.** Those who rise in the second resurrection will be incited to gather and attempt, in their self-deceit, to attack Christ and His people. They will be led by Satan who will be released from his 1000-year bondage in chains (Revelation 20:2-3). However, the Father's plan is to use that opportunity to send them to their **second death** (Revelation 20:7-10). **The second resurrection and the second death are only for the wicked.** Nobody would want to partake in that.

Unfortunately, the book of Revelation and the prophetic scriptures are rarely, if ever, talked about in church. Apart from a hope that they will end up in heaven many in the church are insecure and fearful. They have no idea where the future is leading them nor do they know that the Lord seriously expects them to be prepared for His Second Coming. On the other hand, others are so confident, perhaps over confident. Have they really served God's will? On whose shoulders will their potential demise rest on? Will it be all their own fault or will we have contributed to their downfall?

The benefits of knowing: blessings of the right hand and the Lake of Fire

Apart from the admonitions in the book of Revelation, concerning the important two weeks of world history, the Creative and the Redemptive Weeks are something a congregation can mentally hold on to by giving them something tangible about the timing of their resurrection. One can hold on more tightly when one knows that rescue is very near, even more tightly when one realizes that the Lord will be greatly displeased with those who have not bothered to prepare themselves. Many of the parables, including those dealing with what we haven't done with our talents, are crucial for us to consider seriously.

The concept of the two weeks and His Second Coming before the end of the 6th day can be supported by several other prophetic themes from the books of Exodus and Daniel in particular, including the prophetic elements and symbolism associated with the Tabernacles of Moses and Solomon. One would expect something special and symbolic about the construction and appointment of these buildings and their vessels used in service because, after all, they were the house of God on the Earth (Matthew 12:4; 21:13). Ask yourself the questions, why was God so particular about Moses following the blueprint so carefully for the Tabernacle and why is it spelled out so clearly that there will be a 1000-year rest in Christ on this earth? Why didn't the Bible just say there will be a long period. And why, after the resurrection, does the gospel specifically say that 153 fish were caught and the net did not break. Why 153 and not 154? All of these numbers have prophetic significance!

The Tabernacle of Moses foreshadows much of world history and the pathway of growth in a believer's walk. The Rev Hal Oxley and my teachers of old were very conscious of that. It is a great shame that it is being neglected by most churches today. The warning, apparent in the parable of the ten virgins, which ought to pull everybody's socks up, is also not being taught. Many of the parables, including those dealing with what we have done or haven't done with our talents, consistently bring the same message.

It did not escape my notice that Jesus visited the apostle John on a very special day – on the Lord's Day (Revelation1:1). That alone should wake us up and take notice. He came to give us **the blessing of His right hand** (stressed five times in Revelation 1:16-20; 2:1, 5:7), something those who truly fear and revere God ought to treasure. The **number 5** is the number of grace and mercy in scripture. It is His mercy towards us that towards the end of time He does not want Christians just to be drifting passively along. **His intention is to prepare us by deepening our spiritual understanding so that we can stand and overcome; otherwise we shall become a victim of circumstances and become depressed.**

"But Revelation is too hard to understand. Why bother? All we need is to believe and worship Jesus and He will look after us. We don't need any of that" said a long standing member of the church. Of course, in the absence of a knowledge of the prophetic scriptures and much of the content of the other 65 books of the Bible, the book of Revelation won't make much sense. The problem is not the book itself. During one of his excellent Bible studies that I love to attend at another church the minister recently said, *"I am a pan-millennialist"*. So I asked what that means. *"It*

means that I don't bother about it because it will pan out no matter what". I was disappointed because I cannot agree.

That reminded me about the difference in the dreams between Pharaoh's butler and the baker (Genesis 40:16-22). The baker couldn't care less whether the Pharaoh's baked goods, carried on top of his head, were being pecked away and stolen by birds. His reward for his indifference was execution a few days later just as Joseph prophesied would happen. The story is not there for nothing but as a warning for us. Do we harbour the same carelessness or resistance towards God's prophetic revelations? Have we ignored the 7-times pleading of Jesus in the book of Revelation for all of us to get immersed in the book?

I cringe when Christians presiding over the funeral of profane men and women comfort friends and relatives by lying that *"they are now resting in peace"*. People take the holiness of God and the eternal sufferings awaiting those in hell much too lightly or perhaps even dismiss the thought in their carefree journey through life. The Lake of Fire is the eternal location of the very worst of hell to which the Father apparently gave no key to Jesus (Revelation 1:18). It is a horribly agonizing and eternal pit with no way out, not ever. Selah.

Fortunately, for the redeemed in eternity, it also means that there is absolutely no possibility for the evil angels or the wicked ever to return and disrupt again the everlasting kingdom of God. God will install a permanent 'force-field', so to speak, that will prevent that from ever happening. Hell is securely put out of the way and forgotten, permanently, throughout eternity. What relief and security God provides for the righteous!

I shudder and shrink back when I think about the reward of the wicked. I shudder even more when others who think they are going to heaven might actually end up in the Lake of Fire or in outer darkness – take your pick, as explained further below (Amos 5:18; Luke 13:26-28, Jude 1:12). How dreadful! **We are sadly talking about people who often partook of communion and sat through sermons and Bible studies (Luke 13:26-28).**

The Rev Allan Meyer recently gave a captivating sermon, in July 2021, at Life Ministry Church that might prove to be the most important sermon a believer will have ever heard since their salvation. Taking lessons from his own life, he asked the question,*"if you acknowledge the Lord Jesus Christ as your saviour have you also accepted Him as the lord of your life"* (paraphrased)? His tremendous sermon is available on YouTube.

*"**Knowing the correct password—saying 'Master, Master', for instance—isn't going to get you anywhere with Me. What is required is serious obedience—doing what my Father wills"*** (Jesus in Matthew 7:21, MSG).

It is helpful for my own peace to keep in mind that Jesus said it will be worse for the people of Capernaum and Chorizin than for Sodom and Gomorrah because, in Capernaum and Chorizin the people had seen His miracles and still did not believe nor act on His teachings (Matthew 11:20-24; Luke 10:10-15). Sodom and Gomorrah had been totally pagan and ignorant in contrast. Not everybody in Hell will end up in the same place with the likes of Hitler, Nero or Idi Amin. I thank the Lord that there are different degrees of reward in hell because I grieve greatly for many 'decent' people who have passed on not knowing the Lord.

Any soul and spirit cast into Outer darkness or in the Lake of Fire will be experiencing what the scripture calls the **'second death'** but they shall continue to exist as they will find out to their horror (Revelation 21:8). **Unforgiveness, as a reason for going to hell, will be the biggest unwelcome surprise for Christians (Matthew 6:15).** Obey Jesus while you are still alive: This would be tragic!

Every living soul possesses eternal existence through their spirit together with an instinct in their subconscious that God exists. That is why people all over the world have always worshipped gods of some form. However, comparatively few men and women will be granted eternal life in the everlasting presence of God (Matthew 7:14).

Robyn Uglow made a painting of <u>my first vision</u> which I received in the presence of the elders who had gathered to pray for me back in 1976. It was a long vision that ran like a moving comic strip displayed in technicolour on the white wall opposite me. I read it out aloud for the others to hear as it slowly moved forward. I saw multitudes of people moving slowly forward towards a volcanic crater with a shallow rim. Yellow flames flickered from the surface which created an eerie yellowish aura around those standing by. They were facing the prospect of falling into hell. In contrast, the vision ended with multitudes also being saved. There is, therefore, much opportunity for any who wish to escape such a terrible fate. My own sister was saved three days before she passed away. Praise the Lord!

Nevertheless, the first thing the Lord showed me after my water baptism is the physical reality of this horrible place called hell. That is why I became so zealous about Bible studies and church attendance which astonished all who knew me, including my own family. I soaked up the Word of God like a sponge. Wouldn't you have reacted the same way in my place?

I was very touched by Laurie Ditto's brief visitation to hell. She felt the searing heat. She was a church worker and evangelist and therefore could not understand why she suddenly found herself in hell. In His mercy the Lord was teaching her a lesson because she refused to forgive others. You will find her testimony on YouTube.

Those unaware of the gospel will be judged according to the Laws of Moses (Luke 16:29-31). Everybody ever born will have to face the judgement seat where the books will be opened, not just the Book of Life. This ought to be like phylacteries wrapped around our minds, not to take God's love and mercy for granted (Jude 1:23).

I have always been aware of degrees of reward in heaven and in hell. The degrees of reward in heaven seem easier to explore and define as I did in my <u>Kindle book available through Amazon</u>. It is possible, because of some ambiguity, that the degrees of reward in hell might range between two extremes, "Outer Darkness", that Jesus talked about, and the raging "Lake of Fire" in the book of Revelation (personal communication, Hazel Stokes). Outer darkness suggests to me loneliness, absence of sound, anguish of soul and absence of God while floating around in nothingness with no up or down. *"In space no one can hear you scream"* is perhaps the most classic movie catchphrase of all time because it's a scientific fact. It's enough to make anyone tremble with fear and to get absolutely right with the Lord ASAP (Philippians 2:12). Unforgiveness seems to be a key issue amongst Christians. May God have mercy and give us the courage and the desire to repent. Believing is not enough because James, the biological son of Mary and Joseph, said that even the devils believe (James 2:19).

Outer darkness also reminds me of the astronaut deliberately propelled away from the spacecraft by Hal, the self-aware computer, and floating off into deep space in that amazing Film *'2001: A Space Odyssey'* (1968). It's a dreadful scene embedded in my memory that I cannot forget. However, Outer Darkness will surely be more merciful than constant torment of both body and soul in the Lake of Fire in the company of the devil himself. Imagine what he might want to do to ex-Christians. Either of these options would be horrific though.

I have found it disturbing that in church most have little idea what the **first and second resurrection** refer to. It's just not talked about. Of course, there are a few in the congregation who would know very well because of their past teaching. Those who know never seem to openly share what they know. Yet the Lord makes it clear, in the book of Revelation, that its content is being offered as a challenge to be blessed, to both young and old.

The Feasts of the Lord: blessings and applications

In the religious life of Israel God appointed, under Moses, three major times of special consecration called the Feasts of the Lord as already mentioned before. God considered them so essential that any male not participating or violating its ordinances would be cut off from Israel, for a very good reason as we shall see. The weekly Sabbaths, the **7**th day of rest feature in all of them.

The three Feasts of special consideration in the context of end-times are Passover, Pentecost and Tabernacles which themselves are built on a pattern of **7's** including years of extremely special significance called Jubilees, their appointed times also involving a pattern based on **7's**. The book of Revelation is built on a pattern of **7's**. The appointed times and accompanying rituals all have something to say about end-times. They are indeed sacred because they are relevant for our generation today. The church must take notice. There is no other way of saying it.

"These are the LORD's appointed festivals, the sacred assemblies you are to proclaim at their appointed times" (Leviticus 23:4, TNIV).

THE THREE COMPULSORY FEASTS OF THE LORD (7 Feasts in all)

Passover
1st month Nisan

BEGINS

7 x 7 days
7 weeks
From waving of sheaf

4. Pentecost or
Feast of Weeks
3rd month Sivan
50th day

They were filled with the Spirit when the day of Pentecost had fully come (Acts 2)

Tabernacles
7th month Tishri

ENDS

1. Passover 14th
2. Unleavened Bread 15th-21st
3. Sheaf of First Fruits 18th

When fire came down on Mt Sinai (Mt Horeb in Median, Arabia) after **7x7** days

5. Trumpets 1st
6. Day of Atonement 10th
7. Booths (Sukkot) 15-21st

Hebrew Sacred
Year of **7** months

Adapted from
(KJ Conner, *Feasts of Israel*, Portland, Oregon, 1980)

"LEVITICUS 23 is the single chapter of the entire Tanakh (the Law) *that sums up everything. **God's eternal plan -- from chaos to eternity -- is ingeniously revealed through the nature and timing of the Seven Annual Feasts of the LORD...** the entire human race now exists between these feasts. Let us survey God's calendar in its essence. Sacrifice is the major feature of the feasts. Our Lord kept every one of them without fail even celebrating Pesach (Passover) on His last earthly night. It was on Mount Sinai that God gave Moses the dates and observances of the eight major feasts for the Jewish people to observe"* ('The Jewish Holidays - A Simplified Overview of the Feasts of the Lord', Hebrew4christians.com).

To refresh our memories Passover is comprised of three separate Feasts as is Tabernacles. Pentecost is a single Feast hence there are a total of **7** components to the three major Feasts of the Lord. Other feasts were called lesser feasts of the Jews such as 'Purim' held in memorial of the defeat of Haman's plot to massacre the Jews of Persia as recorded in the book of Esther.

The third and last feast, Tabernacles, was celebrated from the 1st to the 21st of the **7th** month which was the last month of the Hebrew religious calendar. On the 22nd it was followed by an additional day that was considered the last and greatest day of the Feast which included an assembly of all the people (Leviticus 23:36). The apostle John (John 7:1-52) made the point that Jesus attended this Feast which includes the Day of Atonement (Yom Kippur). On the Day of Atonement people, under the Law of the Old Testament, were momentarily perfected through forgiveness by blood sacrifice, the emphasis being on momentarily. The Day of Atonement was celebrated on the **10th** day in the **7th** month of the **7** month-long annual cycle of the sacred Hebrew calendar which God had ordained under Moses.

The blowing of trumpets, on the first day, was to prepare the hearts of all Israel by self-examination and consecration over **10** days before presenting themselves by fasting humbly before the Lord on the Day of Atonement. On this day all sins, including sins of ignorance, were annually forgiven through the **7**-times sprinkling of blood on the Mercy Seat of the Ark of the Covenant by the finger of the High Priest (Leviticus 16).

Tabernacles was celebrated in the month of Tishri, Passover and Pentecost (Feast of Weeks or First Fruits) having been celebrated earlier in the first and third months respectively. **Passover and Pentecost have been fulfilled literally in the church. Nobody, but nobody can deny that. Only Tabernacles still remains to be fulfilled in the church. Therefore it will be fulfilled in the church before the end.** Tabernacles foreshadows the end of not only church history but also of the natural world as we know it. An important point to remember, as already pointed out, that the Feasts of the Lord are chronologically specific. They can be used as a chronological timepiece to calibrate the sequence of events in the book of Revelation.

Tabernacles (within which is a component called the **Feast of Ingathering or Booths, or Sukkot, or Tabernacles,** Exodus 23:16 - confusing isn't it?), begins with '*Trumpets*' on the 1st day of Tishri while the **Day of Atonement** was on the **10th** day, the numbers **10** and **7** being highly significant in the Bible.

Anna, the prophetess, and Simeon shared in the privilege of having accurate foreknowledge of the coming of the Lord to His temple (Luke 2:25-38): The same is happening again. Should we be surprised? Should we not be more informed about the Second Coming? Despite their worship and their brave masks I believe that there are Christians, young and old, who live with fear and uncertainty because they have no vision of what end-times will mean for them (Proverbs 29:18). It has been withheld from them.

Finally, I repeat that 7 times in Revelation, the book of 7's, we are admonished to meditate on its content because **it will bless us.** That's good enough for me.

I don't want to be complacent by sitting on my past laurels, caught as by a thief in the night,

"Keep watch! I come unannounced like a thief. You're blessed if, awake and dressed, you're ready for Me. Too bad if you're found running through the streets naked and ashamed" (Revelation 16:15, MSG).

The above scripture is one of the seven occasions the word *'blessed'* is mentioned in the book of Revelation. The alternative is to be unblessed, whatever that may mean, but perhaps the fate of the clueless man who attempted to take part in the wedding of the king's son, but not appropriately dressed may serve as a warning (Matthew 22:1-14). We need to be fully clothed with the Word of God. Who would dare to show himself at a wedding half clothed? Who would dare to tempt God by bringing up His children only half clothed? The parable of the ten virgins, five of whom failed His will, is closely allied to Revelation 16:15. The number 10 represents a test, to the servants of the Lord in this case.

It certainly seems to me that the Lord wants us to know more about the details of His *"Grand Finale"* because there is something deep He wants us to realize about the end-times that we have no idea of, as yet. We don't know what unexpected things might be immediately ahead but knowing about it more accurately will obviously safely get the redeemed through when it does come. Others in Christ, who were indifferent, will get a shock and be traumatized. Then the Lord, though grieved, will sadly but sternly say *"I have been telling you all the time but you didn't take the time to listen"*.

"Above everything else guard your heart, because from it flow

the springs of life" (Proverbs 4:23, ISV).

It is blatantly apparent that in many churches the enemy has crept in and plugged the wells, *"Isaac reopened the water wells that had been dug in the days of his father Abraham and that the Philistines had stopped up after Abraham died. He gave them the same names his father had given them"* (Genesis 26:18, HCSB). It is not too late to clear out the debris and get the well flowing again in our churches. Churches will have to change. We need to change. We must change.

Part II. Lessons about the Bride of Christ through the Accounts of Abraham, Isaac and Jacob

This section reveals, in type, using three of the patriarchs, qualities in the bride of Christ that Christ is looking for and also the approximate timing of her appearance in the world. Note, in the scripture below, that His bride made every effort to prepare herself. She needs to have something in herself, something only she can possess. We need to desire the meat of the Word (Hebrews 5:12) which will sustain all without fear no matter what the end-times may bring. People need to have a vision of what's ahead and when.

"Let us rejoice and be glad and give Him glory! For the wedding of the Lamb has come and His bride has made herself ready" (Revelation 19:7, NKJV).

Some in the church are actually afraid that the Lord will return too soon for them, saying, *"but I want to see my children married, etc. I don't want the end to come yet"*. They do not realize that the glory awaiting them and their children will put to shame the best this world can offer. Those who express such sentiments still have one foot firmly embedded in the world. How can we expect the Lord to bless us and **heal all of our diseases** if we treasure the things of this world above the manna He sends from heaven (Numbers 11:1-10; Psalm 103:3)?

We shall get a good enough idea of the approximate timing of the **Second Coming** by considering the life of Jacob. Abraham, Isaac and Jacob can be treated as a type or shadow of the Father, Son and Holy Spirit, all working in unison with the ultimate aim of presenting a glorious bride to the Son (Tables 1-3). Scriptures reveal that all three were looking for a bride, each person being associated with a particular revelation of the bride of Christ. Jacob's labours, **over a period of 14 years or 'two weeks of years' of service**, reveal the approximate timing of the Second Coming. What was the contribution to this subject by the three patriarchs?

1. Abraham looked for a bride city whose maker and builder was God (Hebrews 11:10; Revelation 21:10).

2. The search by a trusted steward in Abraham's household for an appropriate bride for Isaac reveals the qualities God is wanting in the bride – no surprises here.
3. Jacob laboured for two weeks of years before he was finally granted the wife He wanted from the very beginning. As we shall see God has been labouring for **two weeks of years** for the bride that He wanted from the beginning.

It is amazing how much the Old Testament reveals, but when we consider that the Lord used the Old Testament to explain Himself to the two disciples walking to Emmaus our amazement turns to praise realizing the truth of what Jesus had declared of Himself that in the volume of the book it is written of Him (Luke 24:13-27; Psalm 40:7; Hebrews 10:7, KJV).

Despite the dysfunctional families of the patriarchs God called Himself "**the God of Abraham, Isaac and Jacob (Israel)**". Why is He not ashamed to be called the God of Abraham, Isaac and Jacob?

Because He, Himself ordained them to become **types or pictures of the triune Godhead despite their failings**. All three sought a bride in remarkably special ways, paralleling the way the Father is seeking a 'Bride' for the Son.

Types and shadows - what are they?

Types, meaning symbols, are used to represent something else. For example, the Passover lamb in Exodus served as a type or symbol of Jesus Christ who would subsequently come as a sacrifice for the atonement of sins. The blood of the lamb was smeared over door frames as a sign for the death angel to pass over that home. This foreshadowed the proclamation by Jesus that He was the door to the Father and to life eternal (John 10:9).

According to the internet the New Testament book of Hebrews provides the most frequent use of typology yet other places make use of this literary feature as well. Adam's sin brought death to all yet Jesus offers life to all. An understanding of biblical typology can help inspire and motivate our faith as we see how God has worked throughout history in profound ways that continue to impact our lives. Of special importance is what types and shadows can predict about the future that lies ahead.

Shadows have similar value. Like a person casting a shadow on the ground the shadow is only a glimpse of the real substance and activities that go on in heaven. The Temple of Solomon and its former rituals, for instance, were merely a shadow of God's abode and His activities in the heavens. They still have much to reveal for us today. For instance, the Bible speaks of the Levitical priesthood as having been just precursors or shadows of the substance, Christ, *"These serve as a copy and shadow of the heavenly things, as Moses was warned when he was about to complete the tabernacle. For God said, Be careful that you make everything according to the pattern that was shown to you on the mountain. But Jesus has now obtained a superior ministry, and to that degree He is the mediator of a better covenant, which has been legally enacted on better promises"* (Hebrews 8:5-6, HCSB).

For example, the Tabernacle of Moses with its three entrances and appointed laws and rituals provide an exciting picture of a believer's walk through the three major transitions in an overcomer's life. It simultaneously also provides a prophetic time chart of the progression of the church from the era of the Law right up to the Millennium which would require another book to explain in detail (*"The Tabernacle of Moses"*, KJ Conner, Acacia Press Pty Ltd, Blackburn, 1975).

No matter where the Tabernacle was located its entrance always had to face the rising of the Sun. The same was true of Solomon's and Herod's temples. The fiery cloud above represented the presence of the Holy Spirit. It also would lead the way where to go next. God talked directly to Moses from in-between the two cherubim on top of the Mercy Seat of the Ark of the Covenant in the innermost sanctum, the Most Holy Place which was cubic. On the Day of Atonement in the **7th month** the High Priest had to sprinkle blood on the Mercy Seat **7 times**. Why always 7?

Centuries later, whenever the prophet Daniel prayed to the Lord during the **70**-year captivity in Babylon he set his face towards Jerusalem where God had placed His Name (2Chronicles 6:6).

The tables that follow demonstrate how we can learn much about the bride from typology of the three anointed patriarchs, Abraham, Isaac and Jacob. They were nomads wandering through Canaan and Egypt, much like we are also strangers and pilgrims on this Earth (Hebrews 11:13; 1Peter 2:11).

In Table 2 we shall consider how they can contribute to enlarge our knowledge about the bride of Christ before we move on to the next table about the timing of her appearance. Fortunately, we have a systematic God who works according to predetermined weekly patterns. This is our faith and it works!

Abraham, Isaac and Jacob. Table 1.

The Father	The Only Son	The Fruitful One
Father God **Abraham**	**Jesus** **Isaac**	**Holy Spirit** **Jacob**
Father Abraham (Luke 16:30). "No longer shall your name be Abram.... for I have made you the father of a multitude of nations" (Gen 17:5, RSV). Abraham obeyed God and led his son to the altar of sacrifice. By faith he trusted that God would raise Isaac again (Gen 22: 1-18). The altar was on Mt Moriah the site of Solomon's Temple, in Jerusalem. The Father bruised Jesus Isa (53:10).	"Your son, your only son Isaac, whom you love" (Gen 22:2, MKJV). Isaac submitted without a struggle. God substituted a ram for his life. A ram (Jesus) was sacrificed for all on Calvary just outside Jerusalem. In his father's eyes Isaac was as good as dead during the 3-day trip to Mt Moriah. Jesus was 3 days in the grave. 	Fathers 12 sons; fathers of the 12 tribes of Israel (Deut 27:12-13). He wrestled with God and prevailed. Therefore God changed his name to Israel (Gen 32:28). He had power with God. The Holy Spirit brings much fruit. 3000 souls were saved on the Day of Pentecost (Acts 2) in Jerusalem. The 12 gems on the breast plate of the High priest who was spiritually responsible for the 12 tribes of Israel. Salvation is of the Jews (John 4:22).

In relation to the bride. Table 2

Seeking a bride for the son	Qualities of bride revealed	Timing of the bride
Father God **in Abraham**	**Jesus** **in Isaac**	**Holy Spirit** **in Jacob**
Abraham looked for a bride city whose builder and maker is God (Heb 11:10; Rev 21:2).	The servant was looking for a miraculous bride who was willing to join Isaac as wife (Gen 24).	Jacob worked for a week of years for his bride, but Laban tricked him and put the less desirable Leah into the marriage bed. This is comparable to the first Adam who was given Eve.
Abraham sent out his trusted steward to search for a bride for his only son. She was not to be a Canaanite but a member of his own family Gen 24).	When the servant arrived in the region he put forth a test. A woman who would be willing to water his 10 thirsty camels. Rachel did not know who he was!	Jacob had to work a 2nd week of years to buy Rachel whom he really loved. Leah had 'weak' eyes but Rachel was beautiful.
This is comparable to the Father sending the Holy Spirit to seek out a bride from members of God's own wider body of Christ (Gen 24).	She is willing enough to believe that the Holy Spirit will perfect a bride through the 5 ascension gift ministries (Eph 4:11-15; 5:27).	This is comparable to the Redemptive Week in Table 4. Christ worked another week to get his bride of choice.
	Rachel was showered with jewels, a gold ring through her nose willing to be led by Holy Spirit. Compare how Esther also had to be willing to be prepared over a long period of time (Est 2).	During the Redemptive Week the bride will be perfected towards the end of the 6th day as was Eve during the Creation Week. Eve was fashioned into shape.
	Rachel was tested by her kin to stay home another 10 days before leaving with the servant (another test). But she was willing to respond immediately.	Both perfected before the 7th day of rest. The bride before the 1000-year Millennium.

The bride in the New Testament. Table 3.

The bride in the New Testament		
Father God	**Jesus**	**Holy Spirit**
Custom of the father leading the bride down the aisle, just as the Father brought Eve to Adam.	"Husbands, love your wives, just as Christ also loved the church, and gave himself to her; in order that he might sanctify her with the washing of water by the word; in order that he might present to himself the church glorious, not having a spot or wrinkle or any such thing, but that she may be holy and blameless" (Eph 5:25-28, LEB).	"And the Spirit and the bride say, 'Come!' And the one who hears. Let him say 'Come!' And the one who is thirsty, let him come. The one who wants let him take the water of life freely'" (Rev 22:17, LEB).
Parable of the king preparing a wedding feast for his son (Matthew 22:1-14). "For you did not receive a spirit of slavery to fall back into fear, but you have received a spirit of adoption. When we cry, Abba! Father'" (Rom 8: 15, NRSV). The prayer 'Our Father' in Matt 6 verse 9.	"And a great sign appeared in heaven: a woman having been clothed with the sun, with the moon under her feet, and on her head a crown of 12 stars" (Rev 12:1, EMTV). Protected from Satan for the final final 3 1/2 years of the world. Why? Because she is dead to the ways of the world. "Then the woman fled into the wilderness, where she has a place prepared by God, so that they may nourish her one thousand two hundred and sixty days" (Rev 12:6, EMTV). (3.5 x 360 = 1260 Jewish days which is equal to three and a half Jewish prophetic years).	"For if you live according to the flesh, you will die: but if by the Spirit you put to death the deeds of the body, you will live. For all who are led by the Spirit of God are children of God" (Rom 8:13-14, NRSV).

Justification for comparing the two weeks in parallel in Tables 4 below comes from, *"So it is written: 'The first man Adam became a living being; the last Adam, a life-giving spirit'. The spiritual did not come first, but the natural, and after that the spiritual"* (1Corinthians 15:45-46, NIV). The same can be said about the two brides, the earthly bride, Eve, and the eternal heavenly bride of Christ.

Creation and Redemptive Weeks compared. Table 4.

Days of Creation and Week of Restoration Compared		
DAY	**CREATION WEEK**	**REDEMPTIVE WEEK**
ONE	"Let there be light" Darkness separated from light	Righteous Seth born after the murder of Abel by Cain Lineage of Cain - darkness Lineage of Seth - light
TWO	Waters above separated from waters below	Noah in Ark floating on top Wicked submerged
THREE	Land up out of water Vegetation and fruit trees	Abraham called out - a solid rock Jacob - fruitful with 12 sons

Days of Creation and Week of Restoration Compared		
DAY	**CREATION WEEK**	**REDEMPTIVE WEEK**
FOUR	Sun, Moon and stars created	Isaiah's messianic prophecies - coming of the light of the world
FIVE	Fish in waters, birds above	Apostles to become fishers of men Birds pecking away and stealing the the preached word Decline of church in Middle Ages
SIX	Adam and beasts created Eve fashioned from Adam's side towards end of day 6	Spirit of Antichrist overcome by Luther's reformation Blood and water from Christ's side brings forth bride at end of the 6th prophetic day
SEVEN	Day of rest in God's presence	1000-year day of rest with Christ Second death for the wicked at the end of the Millennium Jesus has no key to the Lake of fire, only to death and Hades (Rev 1:18)

CREATION WEEK

For a more detailed exploration of the two weeks visit <u>articles (13 & 14)</u> on my website under the menu of *"The true age of the Earth"*.

Hopefully you can appreciate the strong parrallel between the first and second weeks. It is also interesting to compare the two sections of Table 4. The first three days provided an environment and the following three days (4-6) then show what God placed into those environments in the same order. For example, on day 1 we see the Earth hanging in nothing, whereas on day 4 God put a universe around it. God's patterns increase my faith ever so strongly.

Trademark of the Maker: God's angelic and human administration over the ages

Watermarks are often used as security features of banknotes, passports, postage stamps and other documents. It consists of an indelible but faded background image that certifies ownership and distinguishes it from counterfeits. God has indelibly embedded ownership upon the past 6000 years, since the moment that Adam sinned (not when Adam was created much earlier on). This certifies that it is indeed He who has been working to redeem us as His purchased possession.

Events of biblical history define three eras of 2000 years each which can be identified as the era of the Father, the era of the Son and the era of the Holy Spirit (see diagram below). The 2000-year era of church history is the age of the Holy Spirit and began at about 32 AD (+/- some years according to what errors there might be in our calendars). This 'watermark' surely validates the principle of the working week in God's timetable. What is your faith?

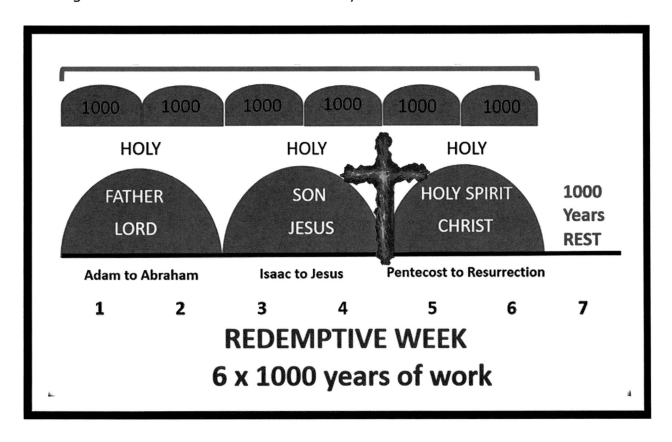

Note that in the diagram each era of approximately 2000 years begins with the lesser and ends with the greater, the spiritually more significant! Thus the natural is amplified in the spiritual.

To repeat, because of its significance, the apostle Paul taught that the natural is just a teacher of the spiritual to come," *...The first man Adam became a living being; the last Adam became a life-giving Spirit. However, the spiritual is not first, but the natural, then the spiritual. The first man was from the earth and made of dust; the second man is from heaven. Like the man made of dust, so are those who are made of dust; like the heavenly man, so are those who are heavenly. And just as we have borne the image of the man made of dust, we will also bear the image of the heavenly man"* (1Corinthians 15:45-49, HCSB).

The Bible refers to four living ones ('beasts' in some versions) around the throne in the visions of Ezekiel and in those of the apostle John, in the book of Revelation. Ezekiel is more descriptive of them (Chapters 1 and 10). Ezekiel describes them as four manlike-cherub beings with pairs of wings. There are huge wheels beside them touching the earth that reach high up into the sky. They are constantly in motion dashing forwards and backwards. The rims are full of eyes. The scene is a hive of holy activity around and under the throne of God. Everything is symbolic, of course. Then we see them once again millennia later around the throne in Revelation chapter 4.

They are curious beings, each of them having four faces, each face pointing to one of the directions of the compass. The images on the four faces are the four icons that ancient Israel marched under – the face of a lion, an ox, a man and an eagle, three tribes under each banner. In the time of Moses the 12 tribes were camped around each side of the Tabernacle in groupings of three under their tribal standards (Numbers 1:52). Moses arranged them with military precision according to God's leading. Moses and the priests were close to the door of the Tabernacle.

(Painting by Robyn Uglow, Mount Evelyn).

The number of males able to go to war, camped on each side of the tabernacle in their tribes, roughly formed the shape of a cross when viewed from above by God, foreshadowing the atoning work of Christ for which purpose the Tabernacle existed – the shedding of blood for the atonement of sins accompanied by other rituals rich in symbolism to do with Jesus, just as the Jewish Passover meal (the Seder) with its readings on the Exodus is rich in symbolism referring to Jesus.

- 108,100 on the East
- 186,400 on the West
- 151,400 on the South
- 157,600 on the North

It so happens that emphasis on the work and person of Jesus in the four gospels have also been written under four themes or banners.

- Matthew: Jesus portrayed as king – Lion, the Lion of Judah
- Mark: Jesus portrayed as the suffering servant - Ox, the burden bearer, chief apostle
- Luke – Jesus portrayed as the Son of man – Man and servant
- John – The divinity of Jesus – the face of an Eagle with keen eyes

Bible scholars call these the four faces of Jesus that have been active throughout history: a well balanced mix of these manifested among men displays the perfect will of God.

The four living creatures, carried around by flashing wheels full of eyes and in constant rapid motion, represent the wheels of administration of the Almighty God that have been active over the Earth thereby guaranteeing the fulfilment of God's Grand Plan for each age of man.

They are a means of immediate communication between the throne in heaven

and mankind on the earth, much like the message in Jacob's dream of a ladder stretching between heaven and earth with angelic beings walking up and down. God indicated that He was setting up a line of constant communication for purposes of leading or communicating the will of God between Himself and the seed of Jacob; an administration to manage the will of God on earth.

"And he dreamed… A ladder was set up on the earth and the top of it reached to Heaven!... The angels of God were ascending and descending on it! … Jehovah stood above it and said, I am Jehovah the God of Abraham your father and the God of Isaac! The land on

which you lie I will give to you and to your seed. And your seed shall be like the dust of the earth, and you shall spread abroad to the west, and to the east, and to the north, and to the south. And in you and in your Seed shall all the families of the earth be blessed. And, behold, I am with you and will keep you in every place where you go, and will bring you again into this land. For I will not leave you until I have done that which I have spoken of to you" (Genesis 28:12-15, KJVA).

The players involved in the four living ones with wings and the hands of a man are a mix of angelic and human beings, priests and leaders, who express the four faces of Jesus in their mandate to oversee each age as shown in the diagram.

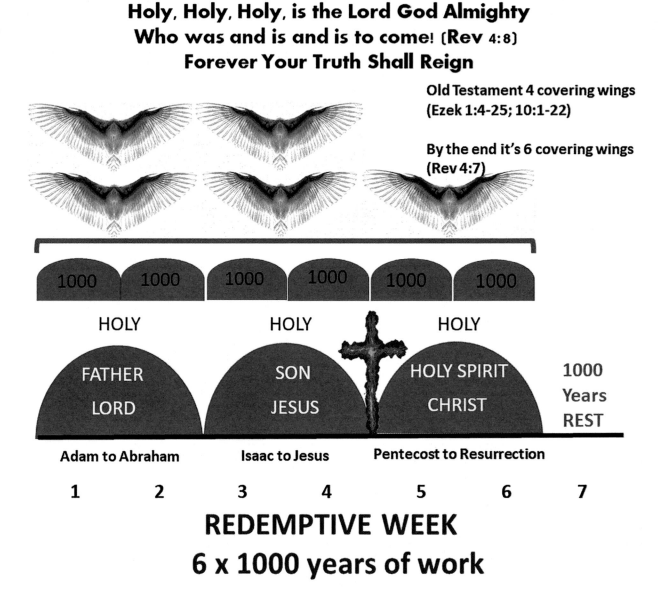

Holy, Holy, Holy, is the Lord God Almighty Who was and is and is to come! (Rev 4:8) Forever Your Truth Shall Reign

Old Testament 4 covering wings (Ezek 1:4-25; 10:1-22)

By the end it's 6 covering wings (Rev 4:7)

| 1000 | 1000 | 1000 | 1000 | 1000 | 1000 |

HOLY · HOLY · HOLY

FATHER LORD · SON JESUS · HOLY SPIRIT CHRIST · 1000 Years REST

Adam to Abraham · Isaac to Jesus · Pentecost to Resurrection

1   2   3   4   5   6   7

REDEMPTIVE WEEK
6 x 1000 years of work

Ezekiel was written at the time of the Babylonian captivity which was the outcome of Israel's constant disobedience over the past 490 years and the corrupt Levitical priests whose sins had become full blown.

As I explained previously they were exiled one year for every Sabbatical year they had not allowed their lands to rest over a period of 490 years (490/7 = 70 years of captivity). God is very particular about times and dates which means that we can trust the faithfulness of the patterns we find in scripture.

The glory of God departed progressively from Solomon's Temple out to the Mount of Olives East of the Temple from where the Lord will also return (Ezekiel Chapters 10 and 11; Zechariah 14:4).

Because of His anger the Lord took the administration temporarily away from the priests and replaced them by angels. Accordingly, the face of an ox on the living ones is changed from an ox (Ezekiel 1:10) to a cherub (Ezekiel 10:14).

In Revelation 4:7 the face of an ox, apostolic, is restored to the living ones because, over the age of the Holy Spirit (the last 2000 years), the administration is restored into the hands of men (apostles, prophets, evangelists, pastors and teachers, Ephesians 4:11), although their behaviour in the Middle Ages was abominable. Nevertheless, by the time of Revelation chapter 4 God is once again pleased with these ministries back at the helm.

In the Old Testament the living ones had four wings indicating that at that time their mandate spread over the first 4000 years. In Revelation they have 6 wings which will bring to completion their mandate over the entire 6 working days of God's week. The wings are figurative of the overarching care or responsibility in the administration of God's people.

"Jerusalem! Jerusalem! You kill the prophets and throw stones in order to kill those who are sent to you. Many times I have wanted to gather your people together. I have wanted to be like a hen who gathers her chicks under her wings. But you would not let me! Look, your house is left empty. I tell you, you will not see me again until you say, 'Blessed is the one who comes in the name of the Lord'" (Luke 13:34, NIrV)!

The overarching administrative responsibility under each wing is pictured in the diagram on page 76. This has been God's most holy plan for our recovery from sin and for slowly fashioning the bride.

In Revelation chapters 4 and 5 we are presented with an updated view of the basic but very dynamic and all-seeing structure of the administration of God around the throne and that which is being restored with the face of man once again on the four living ones. The 24 elders and the four living ones are worshipping and obeying every word of God. The Lamb is the centre of worship (Revelation 5:6). The 12 stars above the woman's head in Revelation 12 and the overall symbolism in the Temple of Solomon, for which there is no space to explore here (but confirmed by a vision I had in Brisbane), are 12 end-time apostles and/or apostolic teams who head and empower the woman through the Holy Spirit, the 'Bride of Christ'.

In Revelation 12:1 she is shown radiating the brightness of the Sun because God is with her just as the face of Moses shone when he had been in the presence of God. Moses had to cover his face because people couldn't bear to look on him (Exodus 34:29-35). His glow was only temporary but she will be radiant forever. Under the authority of the 12 she is shown high and lifted up yet her feet stand on solid ground (Revelation 12:1). She becomes God's administration between heaven and earth, for a short season, as she labours in pain to bring forth a harvest which will initiate an angelic war in heaven and provide opportunity for Michael, the archangel, to finally fling Satan to earth. Restricted to the earth Satan will no longer be able to parade in front of God mocking the faithful (Job 1:6; 2:1-6; Revelation 12:10).

Thus, in considering the entire age of the Holy Spirit, from Pentecost to the bride, there are a total of 2 x 12 = 24 apostles of the Lamb and/or apostolic teams chosen by the Father (Matthew 11:27; John 17:11-12). The mission of apostolic teams is to purify the end-time church world-wide (Ephesians 5:27). It is uplifting to hear Israeli Messianic worship teams singing **"The Spirit and the bride say come"** on YouTube (Revelation 22:17). It is a trumpet call for all of us. YouTube is such a blessing especially during the Covid situation.

Here is a crucial observation about the function of apostles. Jesus is not only the Lamb but also the chief apostle,

"… So keep thinking about Jesus. He is our apostle. He is our high priest…. Moses was faithful … Jesus was faithful to the One who appointed him…" (Hebrews 3:1-6, NIrV).

When we describe Jesus as the "Good Shepherd" and "our Great High Priest", and "the King of Kings" we are not speaking figuratively. He is all of these and even more. As the high priest of our faith He wears a double crown as did the high priests of old indicative of their duties as king and mediator before God, *"Accept their gifts, and make a crown from the silver and gold. Then put the crown*

on the head of Jeshua son of Jehozadak, the high priest" (Zechariah 6:11, NLT). A high priest's mitre was different from the less complex turbans of the priests who had lesser roles. The gold was for kingship and the silver for redeemer. Moreover, as I have already described earlier, the gospels highlight the four 'faces' of Jesus one of which is that of an ox, a burden bearer and an apostle.

Jesus thought of only as a gentle shepherd can be misleading (Revelation 1-3). Even Psalm 23 says that He has a rod and a staff. The word used for rod is 'shebet', the same word as in Proverbs 22:15 for correcting or disciplining a wayward child. Moses had unique apostolic authority in that he took Aaron, the high priest, publicly to task in the account of the golden calf fiasco. The apostle Paul was the exemplary apostle who would not hesitate to reprimand the apostle Peter in front of others (Galatians 2:14).

"... though you should have ten thousand teachers (guides to direct you) in Christ, yet you do not have many fathers. For I became your father in Christ Jesus through the glad tidings (the Gospel). So I urge and implore you, be imitators of me. For this very cause I sent to you Timothy, who is my beloved and trustworthy child in the Lord...Some of you have become conceited and arrogant and pretentious, counting on my not coming to you. But I will come to you [and] shortly, if the Lord is willing...For the kingdom of God consists of and is based on not talk but power (moral power and excellence of soul). Now which do you prefer? Shall I come to you with a rod of correction, or with love and in a spirit of gentleness"? (1Corinthians 4:15-21, AMPC).

I love the way the Jubilee Bible breaks up Matthew 16:18, *"And I say also unto thee that thou art Peter, a small rock, and upon the large rock I will build my congregation [Gr. ekklesia — called out ones], and the gates of Hades shall not prevail against her".* Christ is the large rock (1Corinthians 10:4, JUB).

I am so glad that it is Jesus who will build His church. I have personal desires of what I believe would be an ideal Church but thank God that it's His will that shall prevail. I believe that the awesome, and almost fearful, Old Testament picture of the four living ones described in Ezekiel demonstrates the commitment of a holy God to this administration.

The administrative capacity of the four living ones resides in the wheels for the Spirit of God is in the wheels (Ezekiel 1:20). The wheels were huge and the rims were covered with eyes which frightened the prophet. The number 4 signifies that they manifest the four faces or attributes of Christ to a world-wide body. What else can the living ones and the wheels tell us?

"Their legs were straight, and their feet had hooves like those of a calf and shone like burnished bronze" (Ezekiel 1:7, NLT). The calf's or oxen's feet remind us once again of apostolic authority while brass indicates that we need to have a repentant attitude as we approach this subject. In Revelation chapter 1 Jesus also appeared with feet of burnished brass and fiery eyes that gave the apostle a shock. Jesus didn't like what He saw in most of the 7 churches. Everything about these living ones demand our immediate attention. They link the Earth with the very throne of God Almighty.

Bible translators have missed the rich symbolism which is why some translations call the living ones 'beasts' or 'animals' or 'creatures' in error. They are the ones who are alive in the truth of Jesus Christ.

The primary face of this administration is obviously in the eldership but, after all, God expects all of us to grow into a kingdom of priests (the priesthood of all believers, 1Peter 2:5-9). The smooth wheels suggest that there are circles of circles within the ideal fellowship of the body of Christ that work not only in harmony and love, but also are robust in speaking the truth.

"So Jesus…said, "… the rulers in this world lord it over their people… But among you it will be different. Whoever wants to be a leader among you must be your servant, and whoever wants to be first among you must be the slave of everyone else. For even the Son of Man came not to be served but to serve others and to give his life as a ransom for many"' (Mark 10:42-45, NLT).

"Let the elders who rule well be counted worthy of double honour, especially those who labour in Word and doctrine. For the Scripture says, 'You shall not muzzle the ox treading out grain', and, 'The labourer is worthy of his reward"' (1Timothy 5:17-18, KJV).

It is the apostles who were given the task of labouring in the Word. When the twelve called together the whole community of the disciples they said, *"It is not right that we should neglect the word of God in order to wait on tables. Therefore, friends, select from among yourselves seven men of good standing, full of the Spirit and of wisdom, whom we may appoint to this task, while we, for our part, will devote ourselves to prayer and to serving the word"* (Acts 6:2-4, NRSV).

Ephesians chapter 4 tells us why we need the five-fold ministries operating within the circles of multiple elders - to produce in us the same qualities as they desire for themselves – the fullness of the stature of the man Christ Jesus until we have become spotless and blameless in the eyes of God. Once again, I love the way the Jubilee Bible describes the bride of Christ,

"Husbands, love your wives even as the Christ also loved the congregation [Gr. ekklesia — called out ones] and gave himself for her, that he might sanctify and cleanse her in the washing of water by the word, that he might present her glorious for himself, a congregation [Gr. ekklesia — called out ones], not having spot or wrinkle or any such thing, but that she

should be holy and without blemish" (Ephesians 5:25-27, JUB). In the context of the parable about the wedding of a king's son Jesus said that many are called but few are chosen (Matthew 22:14). That's sad.

I hear the cry of the prophets, *"Who shall believe our report? and upon whom shall the arm of the LORD be manifested"?* (Isaiah 53:1, JUB).

Pharaoh's two dreams concerning the fate of Egypt. How this applies to world history

"The seven good cows are seven years and the seven good ears are seven years; the dreams are one. The seven lean and ugly cows that came up after them are seven years and the seven empty ears blighted by the east wind are also seven years of famine. It is as I told Pharaoh; God has shown to Pharaoh what he is about to do. There will come seven years of great plenty throughout all the land of Egypt" (Genesis 41:26-29, ESV).

The number 7 indicates that it is related to the 'principle of the week'. In both dreams blessing was followed by 'evil'. We can see this principle at work during the Redemptive Week (Week of Restoration).

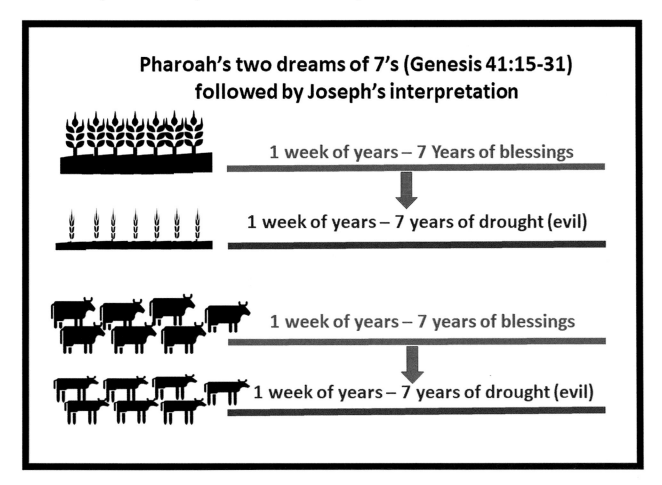

81

Whatever God may initiate, especially during His six working days in the Week of Restoration, Satan soon steps in to corrupt. For example: God creates Adam so Satan causes him to fall. Eve gives birth to righteous Abel so Cain kills Abel. God delivers Noah, but Satan causes Ham to sin (to introduce an evil lineage into the world once again). When Jesus is born Herod tries to kill him, and so forth. This pattern continues in like fashion all the way from Adam till the end of the church age. Satan has and is still ruling over the 6 days of world-history (John 12:20-36; 14:30; Ephesians 6:12). But he cannot do anything unless God allows it (Matthew 26:53). Therefore, it is really God who is in control. Satan and his demons are the scaffolding God is using to build His house.

I know of a preacher who was invited to speak in a local town overseas. The police refused to give him the clearance to hold the meeting. The preacher went to see the Chief of the Police by appointment demanding why he was not able to proceed with the meeting. The police chief continued to hedge and was unable to give an explanation. Finally, in frustration he said to come and follow him. They went down the corridor and the police chief threw a door open and said, "these are the men who don't want you to speak". When the preacher looked at the surprised gathering in the waiting room he recognized them. They were the local church denominational leaders! I don't remember the end of the story but I believe that he was given permission to hold his meeting. It is amazing in looking at the history of Israel that often their most vehement enemies were relatives (Matthew 10:36). The struggle between the descendants of Isaac and those of Ishmael is a point in case. They were both sons of Abraham.

When Jacob (Israel) bowed 7 times to Esau who married profane women to spite his godly parents (Genesis 26:34-35: 33:3) it was prophetic of God's people having to bow to all the kingdoms of this world until almost the very end (Prophecy of Jacob's Trouble, Jeremiah 30:7).

The chronological sequence of worldly kingdoms as it concerned the people of God was revealed to King Nebuchadnezzar in a dream. All these kingdoms have come to pass verifying that the scriptures were divinely inspired. We can have absolute confidence that God is in control of human history.

The prophet Daniel interpreted the dream. The head of Gold represented the rule of Babylon over the regions of the world that God was dealing with. Timewise, we are somewhere between the ankles of iron and the 10 toes of clay and iron which are partly strong and partly weak, unable to cohere. Our current legal systems have been modelled on those from ancient Rome that were characterised by the iron the Roman armies were equipped with. At the time of the Christian emperor Constantine, beginning at about 315 AD, the state-run church restricted freedom of choice in religion which deteriorated into absolute control of the congregation by a Pope and clergy hierarchy causing an iron-clad clergy-lay divide which was against the will of God (1Corinthians 14:26). Nevertheless, God allowed it to bring forth people like Martin Luther who fervently fought against all the man-made rules of the church that still exist to this day in certain circles. Legislation in the political arena is turning against Christians today in a variety of detrimental ways.

However, all that this will achieve is to stir up the righteous. At the moment many are dull of hearing.

All these secular kingdoms have an anti-God, humanistic philosophy trying to accommodate all faiths and gender preferences (Babylonian) at their core, tolerating Christianity in seasons yet with a hidden capacity for intense persecution when it flares up. That is why the beautiful woman calling herself a queen, having *Babylon* written on her forehead, is drunk with the blood of Christian martyrs (Revelation 17:4-6; 18:7). Before our final redemption God will crush all the Babylonian kingdoms to powder, according to Daniel's interpretation of the dream, as illustrated in the picture on page 83 (Genesis 33:3; Daniel 2; Luke 21:28; Romans 8; Revelation 14:8).

Once the Antichrist and the wicked believe that they have triumphed (Revelation 19:11-21), just before the Millennium, God destroys them all with the brightness of the Second Coming (2Thessalonians 2:8; Revelation 20:1-5). During the Millennium the worldly kingdoms exist no more. During this 7th day of rest (Hebrews 4:8-13) God is totally in command. It is God's day of rest and God won't allow Satan to spoil it.

Towards the end of the Millennium Satan and the wicked are resurrected from hell (Sheol, Hades) for a short period (the second resurrection). In their self-deceit they will attempt to destroy the camp and the city of the Saints but the Father's response from heaven will be to cast them into the Lake of Fire (the second death, Revelation 20).

At the judgement it won't take very long to convict Satan when he has to 'front up' for the very last time before God in the heavenly court after the Millennium (Job 1:6; 2:1; Revelation 20:12). It won't be that easy or quick to judge all of mankind who have ever lived.

The next diagram highlights critical examples of Satan's attempts throughout history to spoil God's every initiative.

You may well ask why Satan, his demons and all the wicked weren't thrown into the Lake of Fire together with the Antichrist and the false prophet before the 1000 year Millennium? After all Satan is 100% as guilty as the Antichrist and the false prophet. Why didn't he receive the same fate?

1. I believe that it's a curious form of pay-back God wants to administer to Satan, to the fallen angels and to those wicked women and men of all eras in history who knew aspects of the scriptures to some degree. They will see with their own eyes that God has reversed the curse of Genesis 2:17, that the redeemed are vibrant and restored to health, and that the redeemed have succeeded in living beyond the upper limit of 'one day' (1000 years) which had been the

set limit for lifespans as a result of God's curse ruling over the 6 days of the Redemptive Week.

The wicked will be kicking themselves for eternity knowing that they have no one to blame but themselves.

- **At the Second Coming Satan and the living wicked are thrown into temporary Hades or Sheol (1ˢᵗ death) for 1000 years (Rev 20:2,5); The Antichrist and the false prophet are immediately judged and thrown directly into the Lake of Fire (second death – no escape)**
- During the 7ᵗʰ day of rest, the 1000-year Millennium, Christ reigns in absolute peace over the redeemed. Satan and the wicked are absent.
- **When the 1000 years are finished (Rev 20:7), Satan is released and then thrown into the eternal Lake of Fire, when the wicked of all time are resurrected and judged to follow him (Rev 20:5). (2ⁿᵈ resurrection, 2ⁿᵈ death – no escape)**

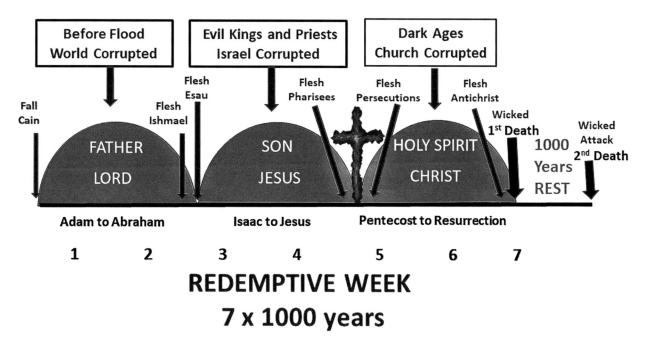

2. Secondly, and from a more practical point of view, I would expect that the opening of the books for billions of people, before the throne, will be a long convoluted process. It's not just a matter of looking for a name in the Book of Life. There are other corroborative books and accounts that have to be looked at (Amos 5:18, Revelation 20:12). I would not be surprised if, in some cases of outright denial, God chooses to replay videos of past lives. If courts can do it God will be able to do it better! Think of the multitudes who sincerely worshipped in the name of false religions. They will want to know why they are being sent to hell. God will show them undeniable evidence, apart from their false religions, how they sinned against their neighbours and the Law of Moses even if they never read it (Matthew 12:36).

During our time with Jesus in the Millennium we will have matured enough to eventually participate in the judgement of the angels, the 12 tribes of Israel and the world (Matthew 19:28; Luke 22:30; 1Corinthians 6:2-3). God wouldn't want that long procedure of judgement to encroach into the 1000-year day of rest. After the Millennium, Satan will be cast into the Lake of Fire (Revelation 20:10) presumably together with his angelic host. Their judgement will only take a short time because God had already judged them before Eve was deceived (Jude 1:6). That is why they are called 'fallen angels'. Revelation 20:10-15 deals with people whose judgement will take much longer.

When will be the Marriage of the Lamb?

We have accumulated sufficient information to deduce the timing of the marriage. What are the key points of evidence?

- The woman in Revelation 12 is pregnant with heavenly offspring;

- It is inconceivable for heavenly offspring to be the result of an illicit relationship;

- Therefore Jesus 'married' her before she appears in a pregnant state. She is already clothed with the brightness of the Sun;

- Christ would never marry a 'woman' not His equal;

- Therefore, by this time the five ascension gift ministries (apostles, prophets, evangelists, pastors and teachers of Ephesians 4:11-13) have completed their task to prepare the bride;

- What had been their task? That *"we all come to the unity of the faith and of the knowledge of the Son of God, to a perfect man, to the measure of the stature of the fullness of Christ"* (Ephesians 4:13, NKJV);

- This fulfils the essential spiritual qualifications of the bride. What are they?

  a. Perfect unity, *"that they all may be one, as You, Father are in Me and I in You;*

  b. *That they also may be one in Us so that the world may believe that You have sent Me. And I have given them the glory which You have given Me, that they may be one even as We are one, I in them and You in Me, that they may be made perfect in one;*

    c. *and that the world may know that You have sent Me and have loved them as You have loved Me"* (John 17:21-23, NKJV);

    d. Another is perfection with beauty of soul and Spirit, *"Husbands, love your own wives, even as the Christ also loved the assembly, and has delivered himself up for it, in order that he might sanctify it, purifying it by the washing of water by the word, that He might present the assembly to himself glorious, having no spot, or wrinkle, or any of such things; but that it might be holy and blameless"* (Ephesians 5:25-27, Darby).

- When would that be possible? Not on any Day of Atonement but on the final Great Day of Atonement of the Feast of Tabernacles, in the world's final Year of Jubilee. In the year of Jubilee every Israelite was not only perfected by the 7X sprinkling of blood on the Mercy Seat but also was restored to his/her inheritance with debts totally forgiven no matter how recently the debt was incurred (Leviticus 25). Note that it was timed according to a passage of 7x7 years in the annual cycles, every 50th year;

- This means that, prophetically, she was suitable for marriage on the final Great Day of Atonement which preceded Revelation 12:1, by which time she was already pregnant;

- This also means, timewise, that in Revelation 12:1 she is figuratively in the Feast of Booths gratified and satisfying herself with the painstaking fruits of her labours – the final great harvest of souls. Harvests involve great activity with time limited (9 months in her case?). You may recall that Booths was tagged with the number 7. Hence, this great work of the Bride is imprinted with 777, three sevens being the number of the Godhead, indicating the perfection or consummation of God's will;

- The symbolic man-child, in Revelation 12:5, is her heavenly offspring – the results of her labours – the 'Ingathering' (Sukkot), the final harvest of souls of both Jews and gentiles. When Jesus said that the Jews have a proverb that it is yet 4 months to the harvest He was referring to the 4 month gap between Pentecost and Tabernacles with Booths or Sukkot being the time of ingathering.

To whom will the Lord appear?

As I intimated in several places, the Second Coming of the Lord Jesus will follow a progression of stages. Powerful signs will precede the coming of the Lord. The earth's inhabitants will be terrified by the enormous scale of the earthquakes at the opening of the 6th seal, in Revelation 6. They will openly confess and cry in anguish that the day of the wrath of the lamb has come. They will attempt to hide in caves and doomsday shelters. They will sense the presence and wrath of the Lion of Judah but they will not see him yet with their eyes. God will be waiting for signs of repentance (Revelation 9:20-21).

All are anticipating His physical return at the Mount of Olives, from where Jesus also ascended after revealing himself for 40 days after the resurrection (Acts 1:9-12), in keeping with prophecy (Zechariah 14:3-4). When the glory of the Lord departed from the corrupted temple, before the destruction of Jerusalem by the Babylonians, it progressively moved from the inner sanctum to the east gate of the house of the Lord (Ezekiel 10:18-19) which faces the Mount of Olives. The angels told the disciples that Jesus would return the same way as he had left from the Mount of Olives (Acts 1:10-11). There is something special about the Mount of Olives where the Garden of Gethsemane was also located. I believe olives talk about the fatness and anointing of God. The fat was reserved for the Lord on the burnt altar (Genesis 4:4; Exodus 29:13; Leviticus 3:3). Gethsemane in Hebrew means 'oil press' where the Father also crushed the will of His Son (Matthew 26:39) so much that Jesus sweated heavy drops of blood (Luke 22:44).

When His disciples asked about His return Jesus answered that life will be as it was in the days of Noah before the Flood but then, to their dismay, the whole world will suddenly see Him. It won't be in secret but will be clear for all to see, as clear as lightning flashing across the sky (Matthew 24:27-37). These questions were asked of Him while Jesus was resting with His disciples on the Mount of Olives overlooking the eastern gate, their favourite spot.

Because the Jews believed that the Messiah would claim the throne of David and return through the east gate the Muslims made several attempts to block the gate. When Jerusalem was captured by the Muslims the eastern gate was ultimately totally bricked up in 1541 by Ottoman Sultan Suleiman to make it impossible for the Messiah to fulfil prophecy. The 'Golden Gate' remains sealed to the present day.

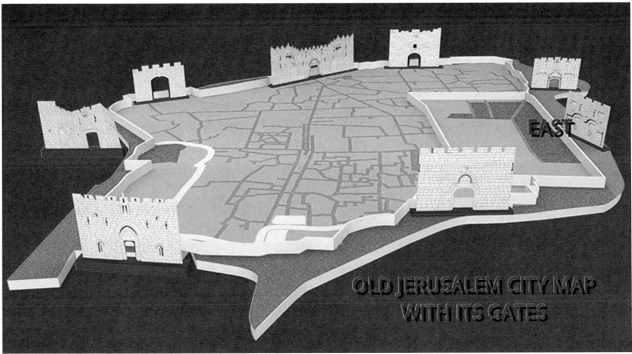

OLD JERUSALEM CITY MAP WITH ITS GATES

Reading Revelation 12:1, of the symbolically pregnant woman clothed with the glory of the Sun, reminds me how, after the resurrection Jesus appeared to the disciples in private, not even once to the Sanhedrin or to Pilate to demonstrate that He had won the victory over death. You and I might have been tempted to do that but not Jesus. That would have made them believe in the Son of God but without experiencing a change of heart. We would do well to remember the parable about the tenants of the vineyard in this context (Mark 12:1-9). The tenants had not only already killed several servants of the owner, who had been sent to collect his rent, but were willing to kill the son of the owner of the vineyard when he turned up. That is sadly the nature of some people. Lucifer knows very well that the preincarnate Son is not only a member of the trinity and that he also made the world (John 1:1-4; Colossians 1:16); but that didn't stop him from trying to kill Jesus by means of the cross. That is the nature of our enemy.

The bride, being symbolically pregnant with child, tells me that she had met Jesus in private beforehand for the 'marriage', another symbolic term. Jesus left us a cryptic clue in Matthew 24:28. In the context of His Second Coming He said that wherever the carcass is there the eagles will gather. As 'divine eagles' (Isaiah 40:31) we regularly eat of His flesh and drink of His blood at the communion table. We do this knowing we are in His presence.

Communion is much more than remembrance. Years ago, when I was having communion with others up front, the Lord spoke to me as I was sipping the wine. He spoke to my heart that every time I drink of the cup I receive of His life. This is why Jesus said that unless we eat of his flesh and drink of His blood there is no life in us (John 6:53). After communion I excitedly told my friend who told me that he just had the same revelation himself.

In the context of His discussion with the disciples, about His return, I can now see that Jesus intends to manifest Himself in the Spirit in a powerful way all around the world as various ones are having communion. When? At the last and great Day of Atonement, the 'marriage of the bride'. Kathryn Kuhlman and those who attended her healing meetings would have been able to tell you that as soon as she walked onto the stage everybody could tangibly feel the presence of the Holy Spirit. Many testified that they were healed without having been prayed for.

Is it in this sense that the Lord Jesus will return to His bride in private but in a much more powerful way than ever before? The 'pregnancy' of the bride has to do with a glorious anointing to enable her to be exceedingly fruitful and to gather in a huge harvest of those with a childlike faith to be saved and forgiven. The Spirit and the bride say "Come!" (Revelation 22:17). In any congregation the Lord will know those who are His.

There is a parallel to consider. When Solomon finished the house of the Lord, and they had just put the Ark into the Most Holy Place, the glory of the Lord came down in a cloud so that none of the priests could stand to minister (1Kings:8:10-11). Once the bride has made herself ready (Revelation 19:7) a repetition of any manifestation of Jesus to His people shall be possible similar to the situation when he appeared to the astonished apostles who were hiding in a locked room (John 20:19-23), but the literal Second Coming of Christ to the world is not yet because that will bring utter devastation to the world (2Thessalonians 2:8). Every eye shall see Him and wail (Revelation 1:7).

The composition of the bride includes both Jew and gentile which is also evident from the great messianic movement amongst the Jews (Judah, Benjamin and Levitical priests) and some of those from the '10 lost tribes' (The Israelites of the scattered northern kingdom in the diaspora), who are gathering from the nations. The initial signs of ingathering have already begun in a small way.

When Paul said that all Israel shall be saved (Romans 11:26) he was only referring to the redeemed from all the 12 tribes (in the New Jerusalem, Revelation 21:12) not to all of the individuals who have Abraham in their bloodline, as Jesus made perfectly clear to the Jews. He said to those who opposed Him and claimed that they were the offspring of Abraham, that they were in fact sons of the devil.

Furthermore, the redeemed, who make no claim to an Abrahamic blood line, have been grafted into spiritual Israel, as the apostle made abundantly clear in his discourse in Romans chapter 11. It really doesn't matter what brand of Messianic background groups may label themselves, whether Jewish or gentile. All those in Christ are Christians who, in turn, belong to *Spiritual Israel*.

Many, such as myself, have discovered, through DNA testing, their Jewish ancestry from only a few generations back; though God is faithful to the promises made to Israel that, in itself, is incidental in some ways, because it's the repentant heart that God is seeking.

Jesus, being the 'Son of David', a Judahite or Jew in the flesh Himself, said, *"Enter in through the narrow gate, for wide the gate and broad the way that leads to destruction and many are they who enter in through it"* (Matthew 7:13, Darby).

The Final Great Year of Jubilee (God's Grand Plan)

This begs several further questions, but the main question is whether we are willing to be ministered to by the ascension gift, five-fold ministry to become part of the bride of Christ. As the Rev Hal Oxley said to me *"too many are willing to camp out early from their Christian pilgrimage and settle on their laurels"*. I had a striking vision of that when the Lord gave me the same challenge and I responded *"I will go all the way no matter the cost"* (see p82, Charles Pallaghy, *'Supernatural Visions and Dreams: Personal Experiences'*, available as a Kindle book or in printed format through Amazon Australia and USA).

The reader might also like to think about how many cycles of 'Years of Jubilees', in the sight of the Lord, will it take for the world to arrive at the final Great Year of Jubilee. The Bible clearly tells us in several places that the Earth has a 'use by date', irrespective of the efforts of environmental scientists and politicians trying to save the world from global warming (2Peter 3:10-12).

On the day of Pentecost 120 disciples were transformed from being carnal and fear-filled Christians to become Spirit-filled Christians embodied with boldness and power. The number 120 symbolizes "the end of all flesh" (e.g. the 120-year count down to the Flood, Genesis 6:3). It represents death to self and to take up one's cross daily.

To enter the Holy Place in Solomon's Temple, one had to pass by 12 brass oxen (symbolizing apostles or teams with apostolic authority, Deuteronomy 25:4, 1Kings 7:25), the two great pillars of brass (signifying demand of repentance before proceeding further, Revelation 1:15) and passage under the 120 cubit-high Porch signifying surrender of the flesh to Christ (2Chronicles 3:4, and p174-178 of <u>my Kindle book</u>, as well as on my <u>website</u>).

In drawing the porch I chose to believe in a height of 120 cubits as stated in the Bible (2Chronicles 3:4) rather than lean on the doubts of prominent Bible teachers and encyclopaedias who think it unlikely presumably because of lack of proportion. No sketches or relevant descriptions of Solomon's Temple remain (Painting by Robyn Uglow). Neither have any images of Jesus surfaced.

Every 7th year was a Sabbatical year, the year of release or the Shmita. In the Shmita year, debts are to be forgiven, agricultural lands to lie fallow, private land holdings to become open to the commons, and staples and perennial harvests to be freely redistributed and made accessible to all. The first reference to Shmita is in the Book of Exodus (Exodus 23:10-11).

The Year of Jubilee was very special and celebrated every 50th year, the year after counting off 7x7 years much like Pentecost was counted off, but in years not days. The shofar was blown on the Day of Atonement which marked the release of all debts, Hebrew slaves, and returning lands of inheritance (Leviticus 25:1-13). Note the prominence of **7's**.

In the diagram the second and third rows, from Nisan to Tishri, indicate that the regular, annual cycle was operative during the Sabbatical year and the Year of

Jubilee as well. The Sabbatical year was special, but the Year of Jubilee was much better because everybody got their lands of inheritance back. This is amplified in the spiritual because it signifies that, at the final Year of Jubilee, when world history will end, every redeemed member in the body of Christ shall receive their promised inheritance at the resurrection.

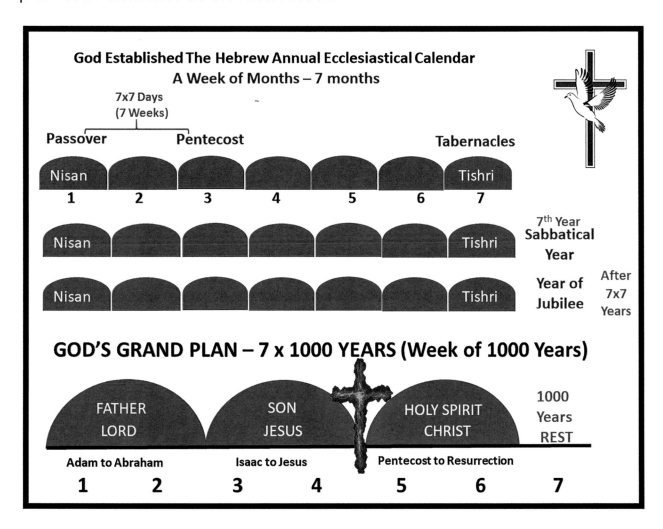

Quoting from 'One For Israel', "The former rains just started to fall here in Israel, right on time. From Passover to Sukkot...from the end of Sukkot it's time to get praying for rain...praising God who causes the wind to blow and the rain to fall, starting on the last day of the Feast of Tabernacles.

Furthermore,"... some would see the "former rain" and the "latter rain" as outpourings of the Holy Spirit... (Joel 2:23). The remarkable signs and wonders that followed the first apostles validated their message...as the days get darker and the message carried by the true followers of Yeshua seems more and more preposterous, God will send another "latter day downpour" of his Spirit..."'. **I cannot see why this should not happen when the bride filled with the Holy Spirit begins to minister.**

Support for a great latter day outpouring of the Spirit, before the end of the world, comes from many quarters in the Bible not just from the Feast of Tabernacles and

Israel's weather pattern. One that I particularly like comes from the life of Samson. Samson had two great victories over the Philistines. The first was when he routed the Philistine army with the jaw bone of an ass; the second and greatest victory was when he killed all the lords of the Philistines in the Temple of Dagon which also ended his life. He killed 3000 in one swoop when he leant, with all of his renewed might, on the two massive columns that supported the building. Note what happened.

- On the day of his betrayal the harlot Delilah (symbolic of mystery Babylon) cut off Samson's **7** locks of hair (Judges 16:13-19). Samson had disobeyed the Lord. His strength lay in the mystery of the number **7**. It also tells me that the account is related to end times.

- After blinding him the Philistines chained him to the drudgery of going round and round in circles grinding grain. The miraculous strength that Samson once displayed no longer concerned them. They rejoiced in the victory of their god.

- Moreover, the word **7** or **7th** is mentioned in the account of Samson nine times. The number **9** in scripture refers to 'totality' and is also the number of the Holy Spirit; e.g. 9 gifts and 9 fruits. Samson was filled with the Spirit temporarily every time he had a desperate encounter with either the Philistines or with a lion. Today, we can have that privilege bestowed upon us permanently ever since the Day of Pentecost as I explained under the heading *'Basic Foundations'*.

- The infiltration of carnality into the church after the initial triumphs of evangelism in the first century caused the church to lose its power and integrity. It repulsed many and became the laughing stock of others to the present day. It is still filled with hypocrisy in many quarters.

- For Samson a day appointed by God finally came. The Holy Spirit enlightened Samson and **he repented** (Judges 16:28). God had prepared this day because his hair had grown back.

- Led into the packed Temple of Dagon in chains, the crowd taunting and jeering, he asked a lad to lead him to the two massive columns. The crowd shrieked with laughter but, when the sound of columns grinding on their foundation stones reverberated through the temple the laughing stopped.

- In this final event the Bible records that he killed more Philistines than throughout his entire life as a judge of Israel. Israel had peace after that.

My interpretation of the story doesn't end there. Certainly his second victory was much greater than his first. It speaks to me about a greater harvest of souls that is going to come before the end when the church is revived. But how did that come about? Samson leant against the two columns, the Jachin and Boaz equivalents in the Temple of Solomon, made of brass (2Chronicles 3:17). Brass speaks of repentance and this is exactly what Samson had done. The two columns speak of the apostolic ascension gift ministries (part of the 15 articles on the age of the Earth on my website) that were active in the early church and shall be active again in the church of the end. In other words, the two guardian columns represent a span of time between the early apostles and the last day apostles, the entrance and exit to the age of the Holy Spirit. The word Samson, in Hebrew, means sunlight or sunshine linking it to the sun-glory of the bride in Revelation 12:1.

PISCES

There is an additional link to a great harvest at the time of the end. When God destroyed the Temple of Dagon, God was passing judgement on the Philistine god of fish, Dagon. It no doubt also affected their harvest of fish to teach them not to meddle with Israel. When God destroyed the power of Egypt at the time of the Exodus each of the ten plagues was a judgement on one of the ten gods of Egypt (personal communication, Dr Clifford Wilson, 1923-2012, formerly director of the Australian Institute of Archaeology).

Prophetically, God has in mind a great catch of fish in a net that shall not break (John 21:11); the total catch being 153 fish (9 x 17, KJ Conner, *Interpreting the Symbols and Types*, 1992). Why else would the world need to know the exact number of fish caught? Nine is the number of the Holy Spirit and the fullness of fruitfulness (the 9 gifts of the Spirit and 9 fruits of the Spirit, while 17 is the total and final age of the Earth in prophetic days, as I have demonstrated on my web page and here in my diagrams. Thus, 153 represents God's total catch of redeemed men and women over the ages.

The calendar for the total lifetime of the earth, 17 prophetic days, from 14,000 BC to 3000 AD, is spelled out prophetically in the book of Exodus by the way (Exodus 12, verses 2, 3, 6 and 8). They coincide beautifully with the Grand Exodus of all the redeemed from this old world (Egypt) to their new abode in the new heavens and the new earth (the ultimate Promised Land, Revelation 21:1).

Many have gone to painful lengths to verify or disprove time charts, such as I am presenting here, on the basis of secular records. For example they pin their hopes on archaeological records but David Rohl, an Egyptologist and former director of the Institute for the Study of Interdisciplinary Sciences (ISIS), has demonstrated in his published works that the standard chronologies of ancient Egypt and Israel might be out by an order of 350 years or so. Secondly, even when using the scriptures which date/s for the deportation of Israel to Babylon is to be used? One has several choices: 598/7, 587/6 (destruction of Temple) or 597 BCE when King Jehoiachin was deposed and sent to Babylon with his court and thousands of workers. There are 10 years to play with.

May I therefore suggest, as others have also done, that it will take 50 cycles (50 x 120) or 6000 years to proceed from the beginning of slavery to sin, the Fall, until perfection in the Spirit (120 = end of flesh). By this I mean 120 cycles of Days of Atonement to arrive at the Great Day of Atonement when we are fully redeemed (Luke 21:28; Romans 8:23; Ephesians 4:30). Please check these scriptures if you are not convinced.

This brings us just a little past our present day, as I have shown in my previous diagrams, on time-charts that have been based on independent evidence. My Kindle book and my web page (creation6000.com) also show why the prophetic duration of the church age will be 2000 years and the Millennium 1000 years, based on symbolic elements of the 'Molten Sea' (Sea of Bronze) on the backs of the oxen in Solomon's temple (1 Kings 7:23; see below). It also answers why there will be 12 last day apostles and/or teams with apostolic authority (Revelation 12:1). So there is much that can be said and thought about or, as Bible students would say, for us *"to chew the cud on"* (Leviticus 11:3).

The challenge before the leadership of the church today is whether the church is willing to hear the prophetic voice of the Spirit and make room for the ascension gift ministries which the likes of Diotrephes did not (3 John 1:9)? Diotrephes rejected the circle of fellowship with the apostolic company and even excommunicated members of the church who did. This requires serious reconsideration, devoted prayer and commitment. This leads us on to the next section.

The Molten Sea and Physical Healings

In company my son often refers to me as Forrest Gump. As some might recall *'Forrest Gump'* is a heart-warming comic film about a slow-witted but kind-hearted man from Alabama starring Tom Hanks. It won six Academy Awards. The film was placed on the National Registry by the US Library of Congress because, perhaps unwittingly, it symbolized much of America's cultural and political history. My son said that I would often remind him of Tom Hanks.

I have a poor memory, but in family circles I would often jump to life after the conversation would trigger an exciting event in my younger years that I had long forgotten. Of course, once being associated with Forrest Gump, the event becomes seared into my memory. This is why my autobiography, written up on my website under the menu called 'God's Grace', focusses largely on exciting things that happened to me.

My memory is selective for which I am very grateful. A few of my past deeds would be best forgotten but they resurface now and then making me ever more grateful that I have found forgiveness in Him. The apostle Paul wasn't allowed to forget his tragic mistakes either (1Corinthians 15:9).

I was born in Hungary in 1939 but, when I was about 3-4 years old our family of four moved to my grandfather's Lutheran manse in Germany where we lived through the last phases of WWII. In the eyes of a young boy I remember WWII as a great adventure, but often think back how dreadful it must have been for my parents and my older sister Elizabeth who is now with the Lord. She was saved in the last three days of her life.

I vividly remember being shot at, bombed, watching dogfights high above and US soldiers clambering up a steep cliff in-between hikes and spending time in air raid shelters. After the war I travelled on many trains as guest of the IRO, the International Refugee Organization. IRO kindly organized fun and mountain climbing trips in Bavaria as a form of rehabilitation for children traumatised by the war. I wasn't one of them but my mother never complained when I was selected. I love trains and especially like sleeping on a train. I enjoyed watching, with hypnotic fascination, the lights outside moving slowly back and forth while cosily lying in bed. The steam trains would often have to shunt to avoid destroyed tracks. I loved the snorts and hisses coming from the steam locomotives, not forgetting the whistles.

My eyes would become glued to the piercing blue light in the upper corner of the dark compartment when I couldn't sleep. I couldn't shake it out of my head during the day. I realize now that it was God's way of telling me that the Holy Spirit was very much active, caring for me already back then, even though I was only born again in 1976. This is why visions and dreams are so meaningful to me. I am a very visual person.

Every time we returned home from the air raid shelters I saw the craters and devastation around us. The Lutheran manse was the only house that was totally unharmed with every house around us reduced to rubble. Even when we ran through machine gun fire I never saw any carnage. Perhaps God erased them from my mind. How my grandfather must have been praying.

It is with that kind of selective memory that I remember two particular portions of scripture from my times in the gruellingly slow goods elevator at university. I was frequently alone in the elevator with the head of another Department, both of us leaving at the last minute to get to our teaching classes. The elevator interrupted for about two minutes the hectic life we both led.

He hated my belief in biblical creation. He always came armed with a smallish red booklet in his pocket published by the Rationalist (Sceptics) Society. Each time he would pull it out when we were alone and challenge me with another apparent contradiction in scripture. After a while I welcomed the opportunities because, during the night, God would always give me the answers. That is how I also learned much scripture. The devil was teaching me unintentionally.

Having said that about my selective memory I recall only two of his challenges, "Your god can't even do simple sums. How come that in one scripture it gives the number of men killed in battle but in another book it says that the number killed in the same battle was 1000 higher"? His questions were always succinct, in keeping with our short time in the elevator.

The answer was usually simple enough as I would discover overnight. In the first scripture it records the number killed on the first day but the second scripture refers to the number killed in the entire battle. That explained the missing 1000. Nevertheless, he was never satisfied and would just go to his class in a huff. He never ran short of questions. Much later the Lord showed me that he had been hurt much in life and was therefore angry with God. I am sorry for him now.

Another question he had is relevant to the molten or brazen sea, I am about to discuss. This piece of 'furniture' in Solomon's temple was eventually melted down by the enemy, just as happened with the two huge brass columns, Jachin and Boaz. I won't refer to them as pillars because they supported nothing. They were just standing guard before the entrance/exit to the Holy Place. The Holy Place was symbolic of the church age with its ten 7-branched candlesticks, as revealed through the dimensions of the Holy Place in the original Tabernacle of Moses (20x10x10 = 2000 cubic cubits. Most Holy Place = 10x10x10). The telling feature was not just in the dimensions but in the articles of furniture in the Holy Place – the candlestick which Jesus Himself interpreted signified the church, the altar of incense signifying prayer and the twelve loaves of fresh sacred bread (apostolic word from heaven). The features of the Tabernacles ought to be at the top of the list for Bible studies because it describes the progressive walk to maturity required of all believers who wish to please the Lord.

This time the professor said that "your god doesn't even know his geometry. In 2Chronicles 4:2 it says that the round laver measured 10 cubits across and in 1Kings 7:23 it claims that its circumference was 30 cubits. That's an obvious error in the Bible, he said, because that gives a value of only 3.00 for 'Π' (pi) the mathematical constant that describes the properties of spheres and circles.

Well, I discovered overnight that the thickness of this huge vessel was a handbreadth in 1Kings 7:26. When I applied this correction, on the understanding that the diameter of 10 cubits was its external not internal dimension, I calculated a value of 3.14 which he couldn't fault.

The molten sea became of immense interest to me because I couldn't imagine how the water was accessed by anyone because of its size. In fact, I had the nagging question why it was there at all. What is its symbolism?

In his book "The Temple of Solomon" (K.J.C. Publications, Blackburn, Victoria 1988) JK Conner points out that the huge molten sea was for the priest's to wash in whereas the ten smaller lavers spread around were for the animal sacrifices to be washed in (2Chronicles 4:6). *"Just as in the Tabernacle of Moses the priests had to wash hands and feet in the brazen laver, so that they did not die as they entered into the Tabernacle (tent) of the Lord, so was the purpose of the molten sea in the Temple of Solomon (Refer to Exodus 30:17-21). Only those who had clean hands (externally) and a pure heart (internally) can ascend into the hill of the Lord (Psalm 24:4)"* (KJ Conner).

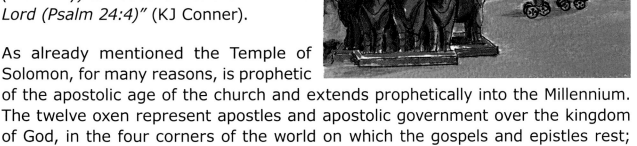

As already mentioned the Temple of Solomon, for many reasons, is prophetic of the apostolic age of the church and extends prophetically into the Millennium. The twelve oxen represent apostles and apostolic government over the kingdom of God, in the four corners of the world on which the gospels and epistles rest; hence, the bulls facing each corner of the compass in teams of three.

I published a detailed analysis of the Hebrew words in my <u>Kindle book</u>, pages 174-179, and discovered that, although the molten sea was strong enough to hold 3000 baths of water (2Chronicles 4:5), it was only ever filled with 2000 baths of water (1Kings 7:26). The King James version of the Bible mistranslates the Hebrew word *Chazaq* (Strong's Number H2388) to mean 'received' instead of its true meaning 'strength'.

What does this mean? Firstly, only priests were allowed to enter the Holy Place in the Temple (representative of the redeemed in the 2000 year church age) and only after they figuratively went through repentance, as symbolized by the various brightly polished items of brass they had to deal with outside. Then they had to walk under the 120 (end of all flesh) cubit-high tower past the two massive brass columns (symbolic of the former and latter day 12 apostles – persons yet to be revealed).

This is why Jesus reprimanded the 7 churches in Revelation appearing with fiery eyes and feet of glowing burnished brass that shook the apostle John to the core (Revelation 1:14-15). Jesus is not to be trifled with if we wish to participate as kings and priests in the kingdom of God (Revelation 1:6; 5:10).

Secondly, the symbolism of the molten sea relates to the 2000 years of the church age and the 1000-year Millennium; 'molten' meaning poured out or melted in the Hebrew. The interpretation is that for 2000 years God insists on us to be continuously washed by the water of the word (Ephesians 5:26; 2Peter 3:5), but in our resurrection bodies, in the Millennium, we are perfected and require washing no further because sin is no more; hence the missing 1000 baths of water which would not be required.

This interpretation lines up with the fact that 3000 souls were saved and given life on the Day of Pentecost (Acts 2:41) while 3000 wicked ones died at the foot of Mt Horeb under the Law which was the first Pentecost, 50 days after the escape of the Hebrews from Egypt. Thus, during the 2000 years of the church age and the 1000-year Millennium believers are receiving life while the wicked perish under the Law of Moses and experience their second death at the very end of the Millennium (Revelation 2:11; 20:6,14; 21:8).

Don't you think that our congregations ought to be told plainly about the gravity of the situation while there is still time to repent? King David prayed for the Lord to create in him a clean heart and to renew, or refresh, the Holy Spirit in him (Psalm 51:10). If we just coast along, harbouring all sorts of hurtful things, heaven will become like a brass barrier and reflect our prayers without ever having been heard (Leviticus 26:19; Deuteronomy 28:23).

It is amazing how many testimonies I have heard about people being healed the moment they repented. I discovered that when I prayed for two different women at their bedside in hospital. When asked, one lady instantly said she wanted to be born again. When I prayed she also received instant healing from a serious and very painful condition. She was on morphine. Next day as I was visiting my wife she jumped out of bed joyfully to embrace me. The hospital had not discharged her yet wondering what to do with her. With the other, an irregular church goer, I had to force a prayer out of my mouth while she looked on wondering why I would want to pray for her. It occurred to me later that she may have never been prayed for at her church or had ever seen people being prayed for. I can only hope that something touched her spiritually after I left.

What about Christians who don't get vaccinated and die from Covid? I heard about such a person who attended a prominent church. There are questions to be asked, aren't there? Do they work up their own faith and therefore arrogantly do not get vaccinated or did God give them the faith? It's a question of the heart and motive, I believe. I asked God for guidance and to prepare our bodies for the vaccination. Both I and my wife were resolved to take the readily available COVID-19 *AstraZeneca* vaccine relying on the Lord keeping all the while Psalm 91 in mind. We developed no symptoms at all even after the second jab. Such things are very personal matters.

Catherine Marshall, the popular author of Christian books and wife of the Scottish born Presbyterian minister, Peter Marshall, who pastored a church in Washington DC, retold their life story in the brilliant book and film *"A Man called Peter"*. Catherine was not healed of her TB until the day she repented and surrendered her will to God. The Lord even told Peter, who was preaching in town, that his wife had just been healed. He rushed home expectantly and found her dressed and coming down the stairs to greet him after months and months in bed. Watch the film or read the book if you get a chance. There are so many lessons there which we all need to hear.

Once again, believe it or not, I had just sent this section away for proofreading when my computer announced the arrival of an email from a lady I hadn't heard from for ages. The letter was long, describing how one malady had led to another even more painful condition which led to another which went on for months. Then, one day, she surrendered totally to the Lord in tears even if it was going to mean hell on earth for her. That was the key to her healing. Amazing that the email should arrive just then; it confirmed that the theme of this article was on the right track!

> ## Does the Lord sometimes heal against His perfect will? Surprisingly, the answer is a strong affirmative.

Jesus forgave the woman caught in adultery, but He did warn her to sin no more (John 8:11-21; Exodus 24). That surely was the mercy of the Lord. In another case the Lord was pressured to heal Hezekiah, king of Judah. King Hezekiah won a miraculous victory over the forces of King Sennacherib of Assyria, although Hezekiah himself did nothing but pray. He humbled himself before the Lord. The Lord killed 185,000 men in the army besieging Jerusalem causing them to retreat in a great hurry. When King Sennacherib got home his sons assassinated him.

But then, one day Isaiah told Hezekiah to get his house in order because he was going to die (Isaiah 38:1). Hezekiah cried bitterly to the Lord to spare his life. After much pleading by the king Isaiah came back and said that the Lord would grant him his wish by extending his life by 15 years. The sign that he would be healed was that the shadow would retreat by 10 steps on the staircase of the upper palace that Ahaz had built.

Now that wasn't a very good omen because Ahaz, father of Hezekiah, had been a vassal of the king of Assyria and was such an evil king that his sepulchre was not placed among the kings of Judah. Anything associated with his name bears evil tidings. It occurs to me that the Lord knew that if Hezekiah was allowed to live longer he would follow in the footsteps of his father Ahaz (symbolism of the staircase leading to the palace of Ahaz). Ten is also the number of testing and trials. Hezekiah should have heard warning bells in his heart.

However, because the anointing of a king was upon Hezekiah, God literally moved heaven and earth because of Hezekiah's wailings and tears wanting to remain alive. Hezekiah was pressuring God into action. God complied but...

Hezekiah had a sad ending as recorded in the next chapter of Isaiah. In his pride Hezekiah showed all his treasures to the king of Babylon which wetted the Babylonian king's appetite to steal it all from Judah. Instead of the goodness God had in mind for Hezekiah, to put his house in order and correct his son Manasseh who would become an evil king, God put a curse on Hezekiah's inheritance.

Are you shocked? God has a habit of doing that when we force God into a corner to do things for us. I will remind you of Israel in the wilderness who demanded meat instead of the daily manna from heaven which they found boring in comparison to the delicious foods they had in Egypt. In his anger God sent them loads of quails which poisoned them (Numbers 11:33). Does that ring a bell when people no longer want to hear the word of God but a style of preaching that is more to their liking (2Timothy 4:3-4)? People vote with their feet, don't they? Churches that put on a great show are filled to capacity.

King Saul made it worse for himself when he consulted the witch of Endor to raise Samuel from the dead. Witches and mediums, under the law of Moses, were supposed to have been killed, but Saul promised to spare her life if she brought Samuel back from the dead (1Samuel 28). God had to comply, against His wishes, because the anointing of kingship was upon Saul. It's amazing how God respects an anointing. That is why David always avoided taking revenge on King Saul. But let me tell you of a modern example.

I read a testimony of a crippled young lady who desperately wanted to be healed. She asked a young neighbour to take her to a healing crusade. She believed in divine healing through prayer. At the crusade the anointing of healing was so strong that she got out of her wheel chair and could walk again. What was the end of it all? She went back to her partying lifestyle while the young man, who brought her to the meeting, was saved because of what he witnessed. Good for him but bad for her!

What is the message for us at the end of time? To pray earnestly to seek His will in a matter and expect deliverance, but not to put pressure on God and wail at His feet until we get what we want. Repentance, repentance from the heart is the message of the Molten Sea!

I shall finish this section with a pastor's testimony from a God-centred church I used to attend. His family was devastated when their teenage son turned his back on the Lord and began to lead a wayward life. The couple would pray for their prodigal son (Luke 15:11-32). At the age of 21 his son recommitted his life to the Lord and enthusiastically began to worship the Lord again. But then tragedy struck when everything seemed so good. He drowned in the surf.

The father pleaded for his son's life asking "why Lord, why"? The Lord replied. "Which would you rather have: to have him back or to have him whole"? The Lord took him to Himself early having the foreknowledge of a weakness which would lead the young man to return to a wayward life once again.

Prepare the Way of the Lord

"For this is he that was spoken of by Isaias the prophet, saying: A voice of one crying in the desert, Prepare ye the way of the Lord, make straight his paths" (Matthew 3:3, DRB). *"For this is the one about whom it has been written: 'Behold, I send out My messenger before Your face, who shall prepare Your way before You'"* (Matthew 11:10, LITV).

I am excited by what I see happening internationally especially through worship groups. It builds my faith that God is waking people up world-wide. Have you been encouraged by the wonderful teams that orchestrated presentations of the *"Aaronic Blessing"*, sung on YouTube in various languages during our Covid lockdowns?

How are we to prepare for His coming? As I mentioned before, His coming will be in progressive steps; He will first come to our hearts in astounding ways before He will show Himself physically.

You may well ask why the gospel didn't start with Jesus reading from the prophet Isaiah declaring Himself as the anointed Messiah (Luke 4:16-20). All the essentials of the gospel could have been grasped from what followed thereafter, but no: the Lord considered it crucial for us to know about the visitation of the angel Gabriel, that Jesus had no biological father, the shepherds, the wise men, Joseph's flight from Herod and the human witness of the Holy Spirit descending on Jesus. It set the stage for the celebration of Christmas and that Jesus was the divine deliverer whom Satan wanted eliminated at all costs. It set the stage for the spiritual battle that would follow Jesus wherever He went, just as baby Moses should have been drowned except for the pity shown by the Pharaoh's conniving daughter.

My point is that God had to prepare a way for His first advent so that we might believe in the divinity in the Son of God apart from the signs and wonders that surrounded Him. The Antichrist will also be performing signs and wonders (Revelation 13:13-14) so miracles are no proof of divinity.

The Christmas story opens a loving and touching door to our hearts, yet John the Baptist's austere life style and single minded devotion give us a glimpse of the sacrificial devotion that some Christians may have to show as we approach the end. Both John and Mary, the mother of Jesus, were courageous and willing to confront harsh and difficult situations. She could have been stoned to death in her village for having perceived premarital sex. Jesus numbered John the Baptist amongst the greatest of the Old Testament prophets (Matthew 11:11). John's father had a visitation from Gabriel and so John was also a miracle child but not in the same league with Jesus (Matthew 3:11).

The book of Revelation is there to prepare our hearts to display the fortitude necessary to overcome a wild cascade of unpleasant circumstances prior to His Second Coming. He doesn't want our faith to be washed away by the torrents that lie ahead.

End-times won't be a piece of cake. We will have to change and face the facts. Once their honeymoon with Jesus and the apostles was over the early Christians had to face severe persecution. Christ wants us to become fully aware of the matters raised in the book of Revelation and other prophecies together with aspects of the timing of the various phases. We need to draw closer to Him in all seriousness or we will end up as distraught and disappointed victims rather than as joyous conquerors and overcomers.

"looking unto Jesus the author and perfecter of our faith, who for the joy that was set before him endured the cross, despising shame, and hath sat down at the right hand of the throne of God" (Hebrews 12:2, RV). *"And they overcame him because of the blood of the Lamb, and because of the Word of their testimony. And they did not love their soul even until death"* (Revelation 12:11, LITV).

There is a cross to come that we have to be prepared for and, apart from the victory, peace, joy and comfort that the Holy Spirit gives, in the midst of trials, there is no other sugar coating I can see in the scriptures. We live in a special but very troubled generation; the culmination and closure of world history in the midst of all the evil we see around us.

"And when these things begin to happen then look up and lift up your heads for your redemption draws near" (Luke 21:28, MKJV).

Where is the Anointing?

King Ahab was an evil king who was constantly under the spell of his wife Jezebel who was even worse. She was devoted to the worship of false God's more than Ahab. The Lord brought a severe drought upon his land in Samaria for three and a half years. Ahab sought to kill Elijah who prophesied the drought, but the Lord hid him at a small brook and used ravens to feed him. At the appointed time Elijah came to meet Ahab's chariot, on top of Mount Carmel overlooking the distant sea on the horizon 50 km away, where Elijah challenged the 850 prophets of Baal and Asherah to see which god would bring down fire from heaven to consume the sacrifice (1Kings 18:19-25). This was brought vividly home to me when I saw a wonderful film on the biography of Peter Marshall, *"A Man Called Peter"*. Peter was the chaplain to the US Senate during WWII. How things have changed in Congress! What struck me most about the film is when Peter challenged his new 'spiritually dead' congregation in Washington DC with a verse from 1Kings 18:21 (GW).

"How long will you try to have it both ways? If the LORD is God, follow him; if Baal is God, follow him."

I noted that Elijah's first action, in seeking the presence of God, was to restore the abandoned ruins of God's altar with 12 rocks that represented the 12 tribes and the apostolic authority of the twelve. Some churches in our community might consider doing the same themselves if they want to become fruitful in the eyes of the Lord. The name of Mount Carmel is derived from the Hebrew kerem meaning "vineyard" or "orchard". The theme I am about to follow provides the crucial key that congregations will have to consider implementing as we get closer to the end.

After the miracle of fire coming down upon Elijah's water-soaked sacrifice, before a massive audience, Ahab allowed Jezebel's false prophets to be killed. Following the Lord's triumph*, "Elijah said to Ahab, 'Go up, eat and drink, for there is a sound of the rushing of rain' … Elijah went up to the top of Mount Carmel. And he bowed himself down on the earth, and put his face between his knees. And he said to his servant, 'Go up now, look toward the sea'. And he went up and looked and said, 'There is nothing'. And he said, 'Go again', seven times. And at the seventh time he said, 'Behold, a little cloud like a man's hand is rising from the sea'". And he said, "Go up, say to Ahab, 'Prepare your chariot* *and go down, lest the rain stop you.' And in a little while the heavens grew black with clouds and wind, and there was a great rain. And Ahab rode and went to Jezreel"...*(1Kings 18:41-46, ESV). Note the number of **7's**.

This is prophetic account of events relevant to the times we are living in right now. I call it *'the Mount Carmel prophecy'*. To enable me to interpret this prophecy the Holy Spirit told me to follow the thread by reading to find out what happened next. Only then was I illuminated to appreciate the whole picture,

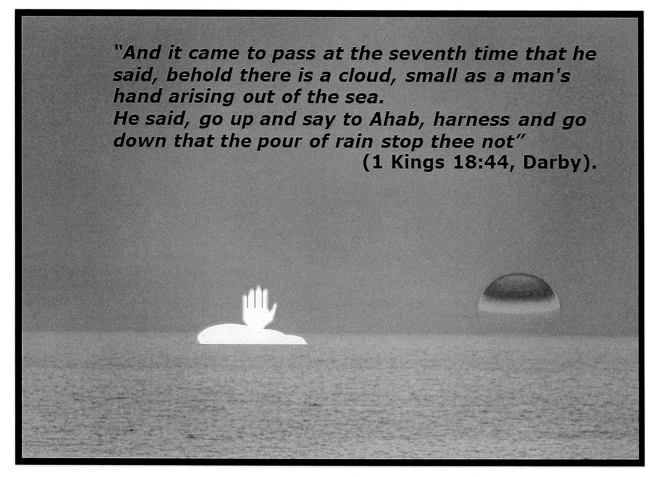

"*And it came to pass at the seventh time that he said, behold there is a cloud, small as a man's hand arising out of the sea.*
He said, go up and say to Ahab, harness and go down that the pour of rain stop thee not"
(1 Kings 18:44, Darby).

An important observation is that the sea was only just barely visible to the servant, on the horizon 50 km away in the far distance. Why didn't the cloud arise from the land close enough to the servant for a better view?

You might remember that the sea is symbolic of peoples, nations and languages (Revelation 17:15). Why would God use a small hand with five fingers rising slowly like a cloud to turn soon after into massive clouds that brought a downpour? Clouds speak of witness and the Holy Spirit (Genesis 9:13; Exodus 13:21; Matthew 17:5; Hebrews 12:1).

Whenever the number **7** arises in the scriptures my level of interest surges because the Spirit prods me that the event is related to end times. Elijah knew that heavy rain was coming before there were any clouds over the parched land. He even advised Ahab to race back home before there was a chance of his chariot getting bogged in the mud.

The interpretation of the prophecy is clear but allow me to develop the interpretation step-wise so that you might believe:

- The hand rose out of the sea which was far away visible on the horizon. When something rises on the horizon it is sure to come.
- The prophecy was meant for the distant future; the 7 times indicates for the end of time.
- After killing the false prophets Elijah became struck with fear and fled from Jezebel who threatened to kill him.
- Elijah fled to Mount Horeb, the Mountain of Moses, where he met with God. The journey took 40 days identifying him with the man Moses.
- Elijah was a man tied to the Law. He himself was inadequate to fulfil the prophecy of the hand.
- John the Baptist was also of the Law. Jesus said that John came in the same spirit as Elijah. John was inadequate to fulfil the prophecy of the hand of the Messiah. He was sent miraculously only to prepare the way of the Lord.
- This is why Elijah appeared together with Moses on the mount of transfiguration; together they represented the law and the prophets.
- They discussed with Jesus how He must die in Jerusalem to fulfil Isaiah's prophecies (Luke 9:30-31).
- At Horeb, the mountain of fire and site of the first Pentecost, Elijah was then told to find and anoint Elisha.
- Elisha was found ploughing with 12 oxen and he was with the 12th. Thus, before his own anointing, the spirit in Elisha was being compared with qualities of the apostolic company of 12.
- On seeing Elijah taken into heaven Elisha was given Elijah's mantle and a double portion of the Spirit.

- Turning full circle we find that the 5-fingered hand coming out of the waters spoke of the five ascension gift ministries Jesus was appointing for the church age and particularly for an administration fitting of the end-time church, **"with a view to an administration suitable to the fullness of the times, that is, the summing up of all things in Christ, things in the heavens and things upon the earth. In Him"** (Ephesians 1:10, NASB).

- Which are: **"Now these are the gifts Christ ... the apostles, the prophets, the evangelists, and the pastors and teachers... Their responsibility is to equip God's people to do his work and build up ... the body of Christ. This will continue until we all come to such unity in our faith and knowledge of God's Son that we will be mature in the Lord, measuring up to the full and complete standard of Christ... Then we will no longer be influenced when people try to trick us with lies so clever they sound like the truth"** (Ephesians 4:11-14, NLT).
- Lastly, it is through the holy anointing of the 5-fold ministries that a heavy downpour of the Holy Spirit will come upon the Earth.

- That is vital for the churches to welcome and prepare.

In short, the prophecy is telling us that special groups of these ministries are going to arise that will cause a massive outpouring of the Spirit to bring in an abundant harvest of souls, the latter rains that many in the church are waiting for but won't admit because of the false teachings in recent decades. Christians want to bypass being taught and be raptured instead any day now.

But why 5? The number 5 is symbolic of grace speaking of regional travelling ascension gift ministries of the apostle, prophet, evangelist, pastor and teacher to perfect the bride of Christ. The five-fold ministry of apostolic authority is the right hand blessing of God towards us. They shall correctly divide (interpret) the word of God. The early church had 12 and we shall also have 12, making a total of 24 around the throne administering the will of God especially towards the end of the age of the Holy Spirit (Revelation 4:4-5).

The anointing of the five was not in Elijah, just as John the Baptist was insufficient for what lay ahead when he came in the spirit of Elijah (as Jesus had said, Matthew 17:11-13). Great as John the Baptist had been he had his doubts about Jesus (Luke 7:19). He was an Old Testament prophet God used to usher in the New Testament.

Elijah was to appoint Elisha as the next prophet in succession. God gave Elisha a double portion of anointing when Elisha saw Elijah taken up in a chariot of fire (2Kings 2:9-14). Elisha picked up the mantle of double anointing indicating the quality of anointing residing in him and in the 5-fold ascension gift ministry of the apostle, prophet, evangelist, pastor and teacher that we need so badly today.

Ephesians 4:11-13 couldn't be clearer even if it was shouted into one's ear.

Our local shepherds or pastors, though wonderful and absolutely essential, represent only one fifth of the team. The five-fold ministry does not come to rule and dominate. Why are they not being sought out or prayed for? Perhaps some have already been. They come to share the mind of the Lord and promote vitality in all members, young and old; to possess and actively exercise their priesthood, both publicly and in small cell groups. The five-fold ministry gift is for the benefit and growth of **ALL BELIEVERS** (1Corinthians 14:26; Ephesians 4:16;1Peter 2:5-9). During a massive revival in Indonesia there were too few pastors so believers had to baptise many of the newcomers and teach them the basics of the gospel. This will become the norm during the great harvest of souls to come.

Paul was not only an apostle but an elder who lived amongst them and was known to all the churches. He often supported himself doing menial work and never positioned himself to rule at the top (2Thessalonians 3:8). He was a tentmaker by trade.

Personal ambitions, clambering to the top and wanting to be 'the first among equals', and retention of power, possessions, status and building a wall around achievements have been the sad history of the church that built walls around denominations. Pyramid-like corporate hierarchy resembles what Satan wants with himself at the top of the heap. Satan desperately wanted Jesus to be with him but only if he came to be under him (Luke 4:6-7, in *"Jesus wants His Church Back"* - the Rev Jeff Hammond series).

In his talks Jeff said that the church is not a corporate organization but a living, interacting, organism. It is the army of the Lord.

Satan envied the glory to be given to man (Genesis 1:26). He couldn't accept

God's choice when he, being such a beautiful cherub endowed with many gifts including music to worship God with, was bypassed by God (Ezekiel 28:16-19). Lucifer therefore, decided to usurp God and wanted to become like God (Isaiah 14:11-15). Unfortunately it is the infiltration of this spirit which still motivates current organizations and denominations to hold on to their structural status quo, unwilling to let go and surrender to the will of God and professing all the while that they are a Bible-based church or organization.

The Lord is waiting to reveal the five-fold ministry as we seek such by dedicated prayer. They will 'arise out of the sea of people' and become His crowning joy and glory (1Kings 18:44).

Conclusion

Various patterns of betrayal will be repeated before the Second Coming when stars (messengers) will be swept by the serpent's tail to the Earth (Revelation 12:4) and before Satan is cast to the Earth himself (Revelation 6:13; 12:9) – these are wolves in sheep's clothing that will mislead the church (Matthew 7:15; Acts 20:29: Revelation 2:2). ***"For such false apostles are deceitful workmen, transforming themselves into the apostles of Christ... Satan himself transforms himself into an angel of light. Therefore it is no great thing if his ministers be transformed as the ministers of justice..."*** (2Corinthians 11:13-15, DRB).

These ones are equivalent to Jezebel's prophets of Baal who have weaselled themselves into church leadership positions introducing carnal elements into the church to make the church impotent, stilling the voice of true prophets (1Kings 18:4). Jezebel, a queen herself, was of the spirit of Babylon who sits like a queen on the 7-headed beast of history, with ten horns (signifying power), that stunned the apostle John in Revelation 17:6 and 18:24. I discussed the struggle to the death between the two queens (the harlot church and the bride of Christ) in the Prologue.

The exposure of false apostles and false ministers of the gospel is one aspect of the church in Ephesus that Jesus highly commended in Revelation 2:2. The spirit of the prostitute queen infiltrates the church subtly promoting carnal idolatry such as idolizing performance and popularity at the pulpit.

"...so proclaim the Message with intensity...Challenge, warn and urge your people...there will be times when people... will fill up on spiritual junk food...They'll turn their backs on truth and chase mirages..." (2Timothy 4:1-5, MSG).

This will lead to a great apostasy, but the Lord will provide protection for His own through the bride crowned with apostolic leadership authority having a double portion of the Spirit as did Elisha (Revelation 12:1).

I am very concerned for a large Christian group identified as the *"remnant of her seed"* (Revelations chapters 12 and 13). Satan will sadly be able to exercise absolute power to eliminate them in gruesome ways unless they and their families renounce the name of Christ and take up the mark of the Beast; the book of Revelation threatens those who do with hell.

Church goers need to be taught and warned what might happen to them if they don't become serious with God. They can't just dreamily float on cloud nine in the Lord just because they go to church and help a little here and there. That is a good start, thank God. However, they need to be encouraged to become joyous overcomers when things become tough by looking more closely into the whole of scripture and obeying it. There is no room for depression and anxiety when Jehovah Jireh (my provider) has promised to look after all our needs.

May the prophecies of Mount Carmel', of Daniel, of Zechariah, Ezekiel and the apostle John, in the book of Revelation, come to pass in our lifetimes. That is my prayer. At the end His kingdom is certain to come, as certain as the Lord God exists. His power is revealed in the intricacies of organisms clearly evident to all (Romans 1:18-32); from lay persons to Nobel Prize winners. His coming to the church will crush all the unbelieving worldly kingdoms to powder (Daniel 2:44-45; 2Thessalonians 2:8).

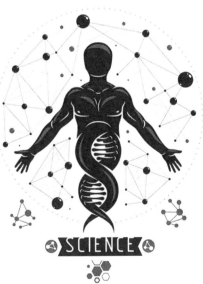

We all began life from an egg cell only just visible to the naked eye!

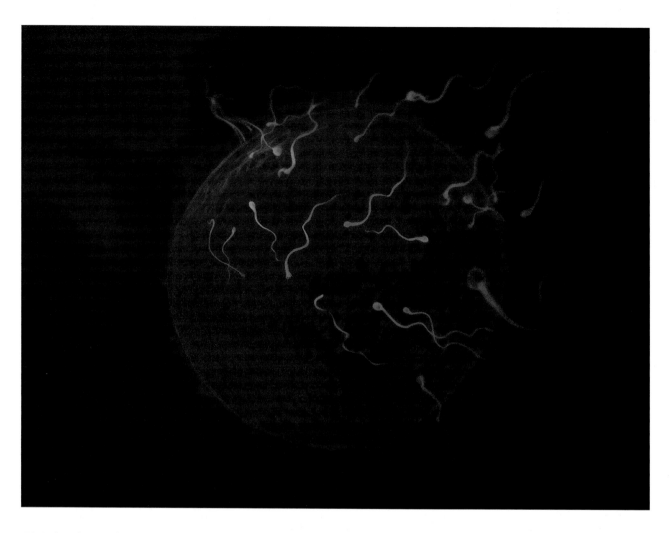

Think about how great our God really is. Think about God's computer program that is precisely written into your DNA. DNA is the blueprint in your cells which tiny molecular machines are capable of not only reading, the million bits of information, but also obeying its' precise instructions. Molecular machines develop the mature body from a single cell. When the molecular nano-machines get it wrong or if one's DNA is damaged, or if essential proteins in a mother's diet are inadequate, then the baby will be born with a physical abnormality. Before Adam and Eve fell into sin their DNA would have been perfect. The Fall corrupted everything.

Think about the various names of God each of which highlight an aspect of our wonderfully powerful and Almighty God. Let God be your El Shaddai – which means that He is your "All-Sufficient God and the God of More Than Enough" (Gilbert Owens, the Sampson Independent, N.C., 2021).

Think about His promises concerning end-times, encapsulated below. Despite the challenges ahead you can make a significant contribution to the spiritual warfare between the two queens. God is waiting for us to join the battle. No matter how 'small' we might think we are none of us are insignificant in God's eyes. I often think, and previously spoke about it at church one day, that a bucket full of water is made from a multitude of small droplets. So is the ocean. And so is the army of God.

I once received an insight or vision; I can't remember which, about the rainbow around the throne of God (Revelation 4:3). A rainbow is perfectly circular when viewed from above. A rainbow is a sign of promise and a commitment by God to remember His own promises. Secondly, a rainbow is best seen against a backdrop of a darkened sky. The world is certainly a dark place and is becoming darker. A simple testimony can be a ray of sunlight and hope for someone surrounded with darkness.

And what makes a rainbow? A cascading wall of fine droplets with the Sun (Son) behind you. You can be one of them. Then people's hearts will be lifted up wherever you go. Ask for a double portion of the Holy Spirit. As you will have observed, rainbows usually come in doublets. Can you spot the faint one to the top left?

"I will pour on the house of David and on the inhabitants of Jerusalem a spirit of grace and supplication, and they will look to me whom they pierced, and they shall mourn over him, as one wails over an only child, and they will grieve bitterly over him as one grieves bitterly over a firstborn. On that day the wailing will be great in Jerusalem...each clan by itself and their wives by themselves" (Zechariah 12:10-12, LEB).

"..."Son of man, can these bones live"? I replied, "Lord GOD, only You know". ..."Prophesy concerning these bones and say to them: 'Dry bones, hear

the word of the LORD'! .... there was a noise, a rattling sound, and the bones came together, bone to bone…tendons appeared on them, flesh grew, and skin covered them, but there was no breath in them…This is what the Lord GOD says: 'Breath, come from the four winds and breathe into these slain so that they may live'! So I prophesied as He commanded me; the breath entered them and they came to life and stood on their feet, a vast army" (Ezekiel 37:3-10, HCSB).

"'…The Spirit and the Bride say, "Come!" Everyone who hears this must also say, "Come!" Come, whoever is thirsty; accept the water of life as a gift, whoever wants it. I, John, solemnly warn everyone who hears the prophetic words of this book: if any add anything to them, God will add to their punishment the plagues described in this book. And if any take anything away from the prophetic words of this book, God will take away from them their share of the fruit of the tree of life and of the Holy City, which are described in this book. He who gives his testimony to all this says, "Yes indeed! I am coming soon!" So be it. Come, Lord Jesus"'!

(Revelation 22:16-20, GNB).

I leave with this quote from Sid Roth, a popular American Messianic Jew and television host, who telecasts world-wide and within Israel:

"When signs, wonders and salvation happen I have nothing to do with it. It is the awesome presence of the glory of God. In fact, when sometimes hundreds of Jews are instantly healed, they are healed while seated. It's ALL GOD!

But watch what happens when Israel is ablaze for Yeshua! And when the combined anointing of Jew and Gentile together in Jesus is ignited by the Glory! This is God's end-time plan..." (*Mishpochah*, No. 2103, May 2021).

Because some readers tend to look at conclusions first I wish to reiterate something I said in the Foreword:

Jesus expects us to recognize the season of His coming. The Bible provides sufficient information for that, but not for us to calculate the exact year of the Second Coming! There are too many variables in our calendars and where exact cut offs between phases may have been. But the patterns are certain and set in concrete. God works in 'Weeks'. May this book prove to become a blessing for you!

We are your fruit, Oh God. We are the apple of your eye.
(John 15:4; Zechariah 2:8; Song of Solomon 6:3-13)

Acknowledgements, Distribution and Copyrights

I thank the Lord for what I have been diligently taught by godly men and women in Bible studies and what the Lord revealed personally to me over the past 45 years. I literally wake up every morning with more amazing insights. Revelation is endless.

Some of the photos were purchased from Depositphotos.com, Lightstock.com and Shutterstock.com. They are therefore licenced to me.

Some images have been included from my Microsoft Office subscription that provides a limited selection of images. The photo taken by the Hubble Space Telescope is by courtesy of NASA/JPL/STScI Hubble Deep Field Team, 15 January 1996. A section of the Thomas Jefferson Bible was copied from Wikipedia, licensed under Creative Commons CC0 1.0 Universal Public Domain Dedication. I also thank Xlibris, Australia and USA, for their help to get this e-book into shape for publication.

I am grateful to Philip Baird for the coloured inset in Table 2, to Jeff Hammond for the cover photo of his book on Andrew Chan, to Robyn Uglow for her fine paintings and to my wife, Milena, for her incredible patience. I also thank Adrian Duncan of 'Duncan Photography' for allowing me to use his dazzling photos of the Milky Way. And last, but not least, I thank my wonderful editor and proof-reader John Seamons for his valuable comments and input.